NOSTALGIC
BLACKBURN
WITH
DARWEN

The publishers would like to thank the following companies for their support in the production of this book

Main sponsor
Crown Paints

BCP - Fluted Packaging Ltd

Blackburn College

Cobham Defence Communications

Elco - East Lancashire Conveyor Co. Ltd

T. Gillibrand (Blackburn) Ltd

Heritage Envelopes Ltd

Parkinson Signs

Presspart Manufacturing

Robinsons Holidays

Queen Elizabeth's Grammar School

WEC Group Ltd

W H Bowker Ltd

First published in Great Britain by True North Books Limited
England HX3 6AE
01422 344344

ISBN 978 - 1906649067

Text, design and origination by True North Books
Printed and bound by The Amadeus Press

Introduction from Crown Paints

A s we enter a new and exciting phase in the history of Crown Paints as an independent paint company, it was a great opportunity for us to support this publication. As you will see when you read our history Crown is a brand name known worldwide but our heritage is firmly rooted in the Darwen area being originally linked within the decorative wallcovering manufacturing industry under the Walpamur company and then evolving into the production of paints.

Although the production of paint may not seem so glamorous, the end result is linked to the world of fashion, home interiors and one of the key reasons for our success has been the ability to predict and create trends in the use of paints and colour in home decoration. Crown Paints has and continues to be an innovator with some amazing success stories such as:

- Walpamur's IFCA from the 1960's - an Insect Fly Control agent paint that contained a fly killer additive.
- Crown Non Drip Gloss in the 1970's was the first truly non drip paint for the DIY user.
- Crown matchpots® the first tester sample pots on the market.
- In the 1980's Crown invented the first one coat paint with Crown Solo®.
- More recently the revolutionary Crown Breatheasy® 'virtually odour free' paint.

As we move forward as a company we can look back with pride on the foundations that were built in a large part by the people of Darwen.

Walpamur IFCA Paint

Crown Non Drip Gloss

Crown matchpots®

Crown Solo®

Crown Breatheasy®

CONTENTS

INTRODUCTION

When we look back into the century that we left just a decade ago, it is very easy to turn into grumpy old men and women as we reminisce about the era in which we grew up. This is where 'Nostalgic Blackburn With Darwen' can help put things into perspective. Not everything in the past was better than it is now, though we cannot deny that progress does ruffle a few feathers and manages to lose its way occasionally. No-one really wishes to return to the days when back to back houses had outside toilets, smoking chimneys cast a black pall over the town, bombs rained down from the skies and we made do for our holidays with a B and B in Blackpool. Still, it is so true that we left some things behind that should have been brought with us. A flavour of what it was like to live in our town can be sampled in the following pages. There are many stunning photographs to jog the memory or to get younger readers asking for more information. Other scenes from days in the early years will bring back thoughts of the stories told by parents and grandparents when they described life in one of Lancashire's foremost cotton towns. Each image is accompanied by text that has several aims. The words are intended to describe a scene, make a wry comment about an activity or provoke a reaction from the reader. This is not a fusty, dusty history book, but a publication that will send the brain and the senses off into a wonderland of nostalgia for days through which we lived or our forebears experienced.

Lying on the southern edge of the Ribble valley, Blackburn was at the forefront of the revolution that saw it become one of first major industrialised towns. Flemish weavers had settled in the vicinity in the 14th century and helped develop the home based woollen industry, but it was in the 18th century that the boom years of textile production began. James Hargreaves, born near Oswaldtwistle, invented the spinning jenny and production of 'Blackburn greys' and other cotton products helped our town become a major force in Lancashire's and Britain's textile world. Although this industry went into terminal decline in the middle years of the last century, Blackburn was no longer a backwater but a large and significant community. It has a long history, being mentioned in the Domesday Book as 'Blacheborne', and had a medieval parish church thought to have been built around the end of the 11th or early 12th centuries. A market cross was erected in 1101, but for several hundred years it had to accept

Clitheroe as the major town of influence. However, all that was to change when the industrial revolution came along and Blackburn was transformed from a market town of 5,000 inhabitants to a bustling and busy one that was home for nearly 130,000 people.

It is the sights and scenes of the 20th century that dominate 'Nostalgic Blackburn With Darwen'. As we turn the pages we go back to the days when the Rossi Brothers' hot potato cart rumbled across the cobbled setts. Readers might recall catching the tram from Darwen to visit EH Booth's department store where they could shop to their hearts' content before unwinding with a pot of tea and a slice of currant cake in the comfortable café.

The companies and organisations which have developed and thrived in the city over the recent decades are many. We take pleasure in including in this book histories of an outstanding selection of different companies whose contribution to the development and sustainability of the city's economic prosperity is a matter of record. With their co-operation and access to their respective photographic archives, we have been able to tell their stories and hopefully trigger the memories of local people who have worked for them or been touched by their part in community life.

It is a good idea to get in the mood for this trip down memory lane. So, before you turn the next page, why not put on the wireless and tune into Wilfred Pickles and 'Have a go'? Alternatively, wind up the gramophone and put on a 78 of Donald Peers singing about his shady nook and the babbling brook. Pop a bullseye into your mouth, pour a glass of dandelion and burdock from a stone jar and, if you must, light up a Craven A. Welcome to 'Nostalgic Blackburn With Darwen'.

TEXT	ANDREW MITCHELL, STEVE AINSWORTH
PHOTOGRAPH COMPILATION	TONY LAX
DESIGNER	SEAMUS MOLLOY
BUSINESS DEVELOPMENT EDITOR	PETER PREST

STREET SCENES

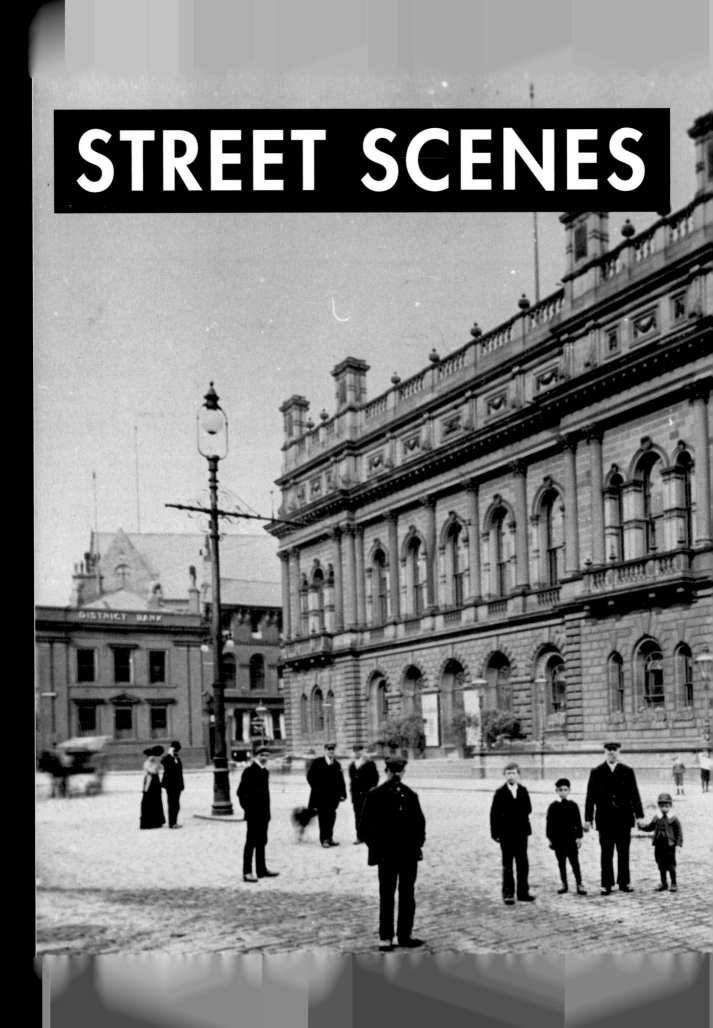

The Town Hall is an edifice of imposing grandeur. Over a century ago, there was little else around to spoil the view. The men and boys on the cobbled setts stood nice and still for the photographer who had decided to use them to convey the contrast between the might of the council building and the small stature of the citizens it both served and directed. From within this great hall and its chambers decisions were made that shaped the lives of the local population. Power was invested in a small number of hands. It was something of a vicious circle. You needed money in order to get power and that in turn yielded even more. Without any major substance behind an individual there was no real opportunity to break the pattern of privilege. Rules were made by the wealthy largely for the benefit of those same folk. Lower classes were given some benefits to help them along, but not enough to help them rock the boat of the establishment. Did those little lads in the photograph wonder what it would be like to have a proper say in decisions that were made that affected them? Perhaps they were too young, but when they grew up and faced the horrors of war in the trenches to which their masters had sent them, then the world would see the old order under threat.

This scene from over a century ago shows the Market Hall, but without its customary outdoor stalls. The children had a lovely open space in which to play. For them, the cobbled King William Street held few dangers. The motor car was not the problem it would become for kiddies wanting to play soccer outside, to stretch skipping ropes across the road or to indulge in games of British Bulldog. Any cart or carriage heading their way could be heard quite clearly as it rattled across the setts. Children occupied themselves with simple pleasures and parents did not worry about them being out of doors. They could happily wile away the hours between mealtimes with no need for an adult to keep them on a tight rein. Today, if a child wanders out of the garden to play there is a hullabaloo if he has not been seen for five minutes.

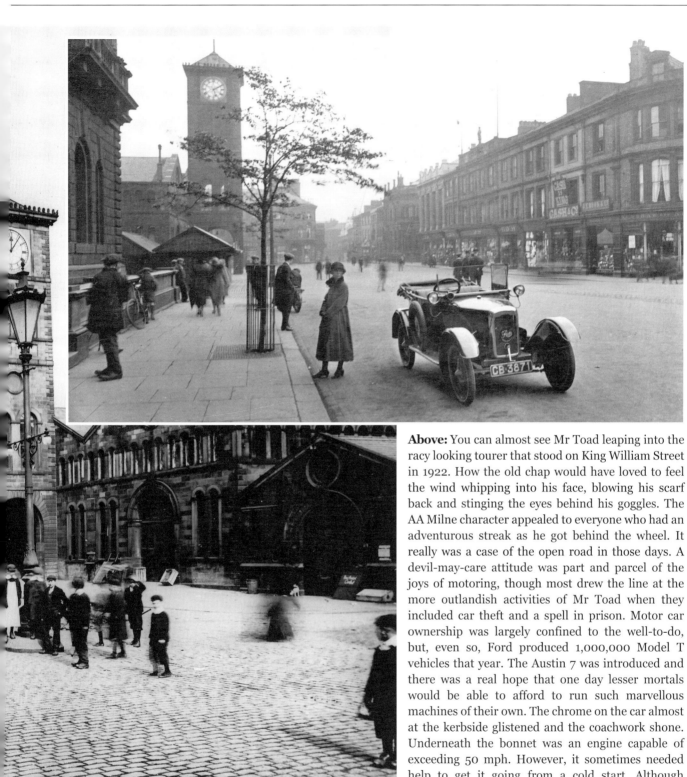

Above: You can almost see Mr Toad leaping into the racy looking tourer that stood on King William Street in 1922. How the old chap would have loved to feel the wind whipping into his face, blowing his scarf back and stinging the eyes behind his goggles. The AA Milne character appealed to everyone who had an adventurous streak as he got behind the wheel. It really was a case of the open road in those days. A devil-may-care attitude was part and parcel of the joys of motoring, though most drew the line at the more outlandish activities of Mr Toad when they included car theft and a spell in prison. Motor car ownership was largely confined to the well-to-do, but, even so, Ford produced 1,000,000 Model T vehicles that year. The Austin 7 was introduced and there was a real hope that one day lesser mortals would be able to afford to run such marvellous machines of their own. The chrome on the car almost at the kerbside glistened and the coachwork shone. Underneath the bonnet was an engine capable of exceeding 50 mph. However, it sometimes needed help to get it going from a cold start. Although Charles Kettering invented the electric starter in 1912, most cars needed assistance from time to time. The handle at the front could be cranked to turn over the engine. Some of us might remember as children helping dad to get the car going by sitting inside and revving the accelerator pedal as he swung on the handle. Woe betide us if we let it die before he was able to leap into the driver's seat.

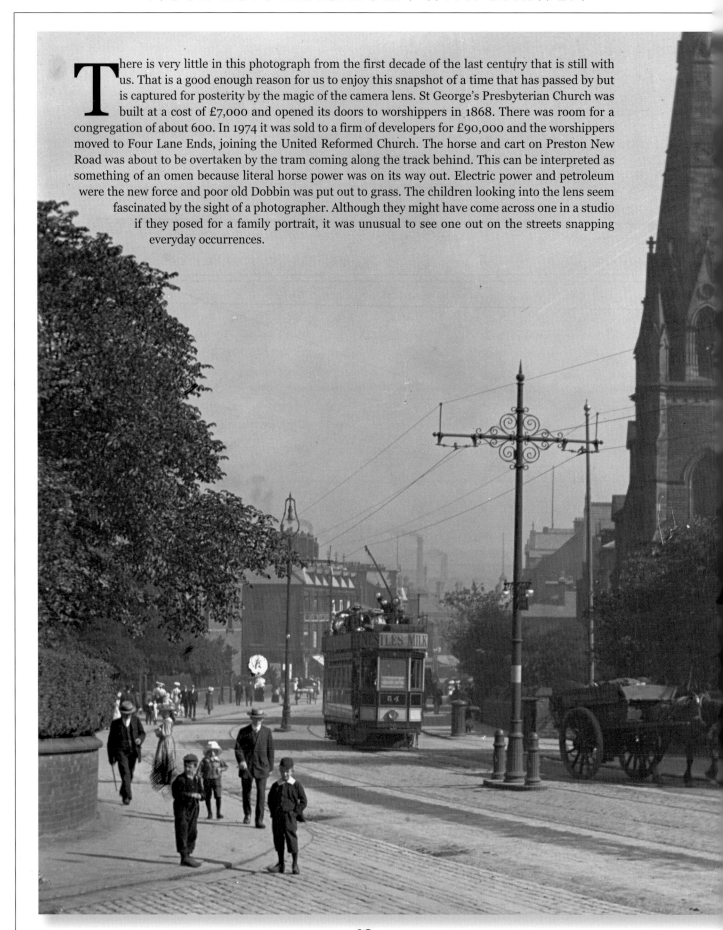

There is very little in this photograph from the first decade of the last century that is still with us. That is a good enough reason for us to enjoy this snapshot of a time that has passed by but is captured for posterity by the magic of the camera lens. St George's Presbyterian Church was built at a cost of £7,000 and opened its doors to worshippers in 1868. There was room for a congregation of about 600. In 1974 it was sold to a firm of developers for £90,000 and the worshippers moved to Four Lane Ends, joining the United Reformed Church. The horse and cart on Preston New Road was about to be overtaken by the tram coming along the track behind. This can be interpreted as something of an omen because literal horse power was on its way out. Electric power and petroleum were the new force and poor old Dobbin was put out to grass. The children looking into the lens seem fascinated by the sight of a photographer. Although they might have come across one in a studio if they posed for a family portrait, it was unusual to see one out on the streets snapping everyday occurrences.

Below: The smartly turned out Edwardian lady outside the Town Hall had her attention taken by an example of the very latest fashion in modern transport. Would it ever catch on? The first motor cars were not for the faint hearted as they could bowl along merrily without too much in the way of safety devices. While pedestrians were at risk, it was the danger to horses and the passengers in the carriages they pulled that concerned the authorities. They were frightened that the animals might be spooked with catastrophic results. At first, a motor car had to have someone walking in front of it brandishing a red flag as a warning. The speed limit was 4 mph on the open road and a mere 2 mph in towns. This was obviously ridiculous and the measure was repealed in 1896 and a new restriction set at 12 mph. Needless to say, requirement for the man with the red flag was abolished as no-one could be expected to run a five minute mile infront of a car. However, with the advance in technology a more realistic limit was set at 20 mph in 1903. Driving licences, but not tests, and registration numbers were also introduced at this time.

Below: The official opening of the Victoria Tower, Darwen, by the Lord of the Manor, the Rev WA Duckworth, took place on 24th September 1898, when a huge celebration bonfire was lit to mark the occasion. Standing 1,225ft above sea level, the 86ft landmark was the towns tribute to Queen Victoria's Diamond Jubliee in June 1887, with £700 being raised for its construction by public donations. It took over a year to build. The metal glass dome at the top of the tower was blown off in a gale in 1947, it was replaced with a replica in 1972.

Above: Darwen, or Over Darwen as it was formerly called, was incorporated as a municipal borough in 1878. The town had grown rapidly in the mid 19th century from a modest hamlet to sizeable population centre. Its first purpose built market, the Greenway, was built with private capital by Eccles Shorrock in 1847. However, bigger and better facilities were needed to compete with neighbouring Blackburn. The Market Hall and Municipal Offices seen here were opened in 1871 and the square fronting them was well used by traders selling their wares. On days when important announcements were made, members of the local community would gather there to be addressed by the Mayor or some other dignitary.

Left: Have no fear. This is not evidence of a siege of Darwen Market Hall. The local Rifle Volunteers were firing a celebratory volley or 'feu de joie' to mark the cutting of the first sod in preparation for the building of Darwen Tower. Sometimes referred to in disparaging terms as 'the pepper pot', it was erected in Bold Venture Park to mark Queen Victoria's Golden Jubilee. To many, it also represented the freeing of Darwen Moor the year before from the feudal control of William Duckworth, the landowner who had blocked ancient rights of way across his land. As well as presiding at this photographed gathering, Mayor Alexander Carus dug the first spadeful of earth at the site of the Tower in front of a crowd of over 3,000 on 22 June 1897, though it took over a year in completion.

sight of dive bombers of the German Condor Squadrons razing to the ground the picturesque, historical Basque village of Guernica was enough to make the blood freeze. After the Germans marched into Poland, Britain was on the alert, but as the months rolled by things at home seemed to be continuing with some sort of normality. But we had been lulled into a false sense of security. In the summer of 1940 the skies were filled with aeroplanes. The Battle of Britain began and the German blitz on our towns and cities started in earnest. This photograph of Ainsworth Street shows some of the extensive damage caused by the bombs that fell on 31 August. The war against the civilian population was now on.

Below: Back with a vengeance. Just two days after Darwen's first air-raid, the luftwaffe returned. During a sneak daylight raid on 21st October 1940, three bombs were dropped in a town centre backstreet, flattening houses in Crown Street and Holme Street. The plane also machine-gunned a Corporation bus as it sped away. Six people were killed instantly and a seventh died from injuries five months later. Here firemen are seen in a bomb crater in Crown Street.

Above: As the storm clouds of war gathered on the horizon in 1939, urgent work was carried out in setting up our defences against what was certain to be a vicious and hurtful period of hostilities. Preparations were made to issue gasmasks to schoolchildren and for their evacuation once war was declared. Civil defence groups organised emergency drills and measures were taken to protect us from invasion, but the biggest effort was devoted to air raid precautions. Large anti aircraft guns were commissioned, shelters constructed, rescue services augmented and instructions given to the public on how to respond when the sirens were sounded. Most were aware of the nature of modern aerial warfare. It was going to be different from the Great War, if the experience of the Spanish Civil War was any portent. The

Below: Local wags give nicknames to buildings and places that inspire either affection or distaste. 'Paddy's wigwam' is the name given by Scousers to Liverpool's modern looking Catholic Cathedral. Dubliners refer to the millennium needle on O'Connell Street as the 'stiletto in the ghetto'. Closer to home, Darwen residents referred to the Royal Liver Friendly Society building as the 'Potted Meat Bank'. This was not a reference to the building being shaped like a jar of Shippam's paste, but to a play on the pronunciation and meaning of the word 'liver'. Pictured just a few years before the First World War, this financial institution had been founded on Merseyside in 1850 as the Liverpool Lyver Burial Society. As suggested by its name, it was established to fund funerals and save families from financial hardship when a wage earning relative passed away. It evolved into the Royal Liver in 1907. By then, its influence had spread nationwide. A friendly or mutual society is owned by its members rather than shareholders, namely those who take out a policy. The two elegant ladies on the right probably did not have any need for such an establishment as their husbands would put their money into banks, stocks and shares. But for the less well heeled, the friendly societies provided a way of making modest payments that would protect their families in times of need.

This page: The British are supposed to have a fixation with the weather and are accused by outsiders of having little else to talk about. It must be admitted that even our musical tastes can be influenced by meteorology and, looking at this scene, memories of Jane Morgan's 1958 hit 'The day that the rains came down' or The Cascades, five years later, singing about the 'Rhythm of the rain' come flooding back, to coin an apt term. This dramatic scene was recorded on Princess Street in the suitably named Waterfall district. The police worked hard getting to people marooned in bedrooms and helped some get way from the scene by lifting them bodily onto the back of a special rescue lorry. Although the incursion of water into homes and businesses damages property and possessions, it is the aftermath that is even worse. The cleaning up operation is as prolonged as the stench that accompanies each occurrence. After any flood there is also a real danger of disease. Children are prone to splash around in the filthy water that gathers in the street, thinking it a lark, oblivious to the dangers of what germs and bacteria lie within those murky depths. At least most of the residents on the street were friendly and neighbourly, as was often the case in working class communities who lived in the traditional terraced properties. They would chip in with some meaningful contributions where they could.

The Bay Horse on Salford, seen at the junction with Church Street and Ainsworth Street was a Thwaites hostelry. The famous shire horses belonging to the brewery were once an attractive sight here as they pulled their drays laden with casks of best bitter. Daniel Thwaites began in business in 1807 and the Blackburn company has been at the forefront of good supping ever since. Cinema goers often warmed up for an evening at the pictures with a drink in the Bay Horse before crossing the road to the Royal Cinema where the 1949 movie 'Hasty Heart', starring Richard Todd and Patricia Neal, was the main attraction. A certain Ronald Reagan played a supporting part and we would hear more about him 30 years later. Todd became a well respected screen actor and is particularly remembered for his role as Guy Gibson in 'The

Dambusters'. The crew of the bus to Brownhill passed the time of day with one another, while the Wilpshire bound conductor fielded a query from a couple of passengers. Either that or he was chatting them up. Behind them, on the corner of New Water Street, there are a couple of interesting adverts in the window of the newsagents. Dora Wilson's School of Dancing was part of the modern culture at a time when everyone needed to learn the art of the waltz and the rumba.

Sherman's Pools, a Cardiff based company, was one of the big names in football betting, along with Littlewood's, Vernon's, Cope's and Zetters. The photograph is a true period piece from the middle of the last century capturing a cobbled highway, wrought iron lamppost and studded pedestrian crossing. It was taken when every town had a flourishing Woolworth's. Who, then, could ever have seen that chain of stores fall by the wayside?

Below: Blackburn has some hilly parts to it. If that was not obvious then you only have to look at this view across the town centre taken from Balaclava Street. Just a few yards away, we could come across Inkerman Street. The Victorians enjoyed naming streets after famous figures and occasions from the recent past. The Battle of Inkerman in 1854 saw a combined force of British and French troops defeat a Russian army during the Crimean War. It took place just a month after the famous Charge of the Light Brigade during the Battle of Balaclava. In this photograph, the Town Hall tower can be seen clearly, but the cupola style adornment to the roof on the left is of more interest to someone observing the changing face of the town. This area has seen a significant rise in the number of families living here who have an Asian background. Some buildings, including former churches, have been turned into mosques as those Islamic followers sought their own places of worship.

Left: He stood at the bottom of Limbrick for over half a century, gazing down upon the passers-by who live in the town he helped to shape. William Henry Hornby (1805-84) came into this world around the time that Nelson was fighting the Battle of Trafalgar. His life mirrored the growth of his home town as it developed from its infancy in the industrial revolution to a figure of great importance in the world of commerce. By the time that Blackburn achieved borough status, Hornby was one of the town's major employers. He became our first ever Mayor in 1851 and moved onto a more elevated political status when he was elected to Parliament in 1857. He served as one of our MPs until 1865. The statue was erected in his memory in 1912. Modelled in bronze and showing him with his walking cane in hand, it was presented to the people of Blackburn by John Margerison who worked at Hornby's Brookhouse Mills for more than 50 years. The statue was taken down in 1968 during the regeneration of this part of town. It was later brought out of storage and erected in an appropriate position near the old Town Hall in King William Mall, where it was unveiled on 17 June, 1970. One of Hornby's sons has a sporting claim to fame, or should that be infamy? Albert Hornby was the England cricket captain in the 1882 Test match against Australia when the Ashes were created after our ignominious defeat...

Just for a moment you might be fooled into thinking that this is some sort of practice area for a new event in the Winter Olympics. There is a bit of snow on the ground, but the vehicle heading down the ramp is on wheels rather than skis. Even the most imaginative reader could hardly see Eddie the Eagle whizzing down here as he soars into space and into his quite individual style of jump. Not for us the delights of a ski slope, though you only have to go to Whalley or Rossendale to indulge yourself if that is how your fancy strikes you. This concrete bridge was actually part of the first phase in the redevelopment of the town centre. The ramp led up to a car park above the new shopping centre that was being constructed on the site of the old market place. Before the curves were straightened into one long section, this part swept along from Victoria Street, crossing the former hen market and Town Hall Street. The market was held on a cobbled part of the area behind the old Town Hall. Back in the interwar years, many people kept hens in pens in their back yards. At this market you could also see linnets, skylarks and canaries all in cages and ready to be sold to householders wanting something tuneful as well as decorative in their front parlours.

Right and below: The Boulevard was a busy place in the 1950s with the bus stands outside the railway station packed with people waiting to get on board. Nowadays, this link between two forms of public transport is referred to as an interchange. The history of public transport on Blackburn's roads goes back to 1881 when the Blackburn and Over Darwen Tramways Company ran the steam trams that served the district. After the respective councils took over the administration of the electrified routes around the turn of the century, the trams provided a reliable

service for everyone in the area. It was not until the end of the 1920s that petrol engine buses were introduced. Leyland Tigers and Titans formed the nucleus of the first fleet that was put into service. After the last war Blackburn Corporation bought 83 new buses to replace the tramcars that had been phased out by 1949. Many of those can be seen in these photographs as no new ones

were purchased for seven more years. The largely green livery was a distinctive sight on the borough's roads.

All the double deckers were crewed in pairs by a driver and conductor. The latter collected the cash and gave out the tickets, leaving his partner to attend to the road. Marooned in his cab, the driver relied on the conductor's use of the bell to indicate when to stop or move off. Three rings meant that the bus was full and it could whiz happily past a bus stop where irate potential passengers were left behind in utter frustration. Although women often drove the vehicles in wartime, they were nearly all relegated to the role of clippies in peacetime. They developed good social skills dealing with the general public, especially the cheeky young men who were not afraid to ask an attractive conductress, 'How far will you go for two bob, love?'

After reorganisation in 1974, the paintwork was changed to having just green at the bottom of the bus bodies. Later, this changed to white with a red roof, reflecting part of the colours of Darwen Transport that had been incorporated into the new Borough of Blackburn Transport Company. The new livery was unpopular and, in 1983, the traditional green was reinstated. However, the tinkering continued and cream with green bands was introduced in 1990. Deregulation and ownership changes meant that Blackburn's bus service lost much of its own identity. Eventually, in 2007, the business came into the hands of Lancashire United.

Below and right: Parking on the rooftop on Ainsworth Street meant that there was plenty of space for cinemagoers who wanted to spend some time at the Odeon on Penny Street. The former Rialto was in a sorry state by the time of its demolition in the 1970s and a far cry from the opulent pleasure palace that it once had been. Taken over and renamed in the late 1950s, it came under the wing of a group that was founded in Dudley in 1928 by Oscar Deutsch, the son of a Hungarian Jewish scrap merchant. 'Odeon' is supposed to stand for 'Oscar Deutsch entertains our nation', though whether this preceded or followed the naming is a matter of some debate. Whatever the circumstances, Deutsch opened 250 cinemas in the 1930s, the heydays of the movies. After his death in 1941, his widow sold out to J Arthur

Rank, but the name was retained. Going to the pictures, as we called it, had another lease of life after the war. These were wonderful times. Cuddling up with a sweetheart on the back row and dodging the usherette's torchlight when things got amorous was all part of a good Saturday night out. The scramble for the exit when 'God save the king' was played at the end, trampling over the more patriotic punters who stayed put, was also traditional behaviour for many.

EVENTS & OCCASIONS

Padiham County Primary School had its own celebrations on Coronation Day and teachers, mums and dinner ladies joined in the fun. The grub made a change from the usual school dinner of lumpy spuds, tough meat, bullet peas and revolting tapioca, or frogspawn as the children referred to it. The kiddies in the photograph were the baby boomers, born just after the war when the birthrate rocketed. When the menfolk returned from service overseas they and their long suffering wives did what came naturally and the stork put in a claim for overtime. By now, those preparing to tuck in will have exchanged their meal tickets for bus passes, but we can be sure that they still remember the day when they shouted 'Hip-hip-hooray' for Her Majesty and played royal musical thrones in the assembly hall.

Left: Considering that it was taken in 1882, this photograph is in remarkable condition, showing quite clearly the hordes of children in the foreground and the adults above. Gathered by the Lancashire and Yorkshire Bank, in front of the Theatre Royal, everyone had come to witness the grand opening of Darwen Market Hall. The ceremony should have taken place in May, but was postponed following the assassination of Lord Frederick Cavendish in Phoenix Park, Dublin. He was the brother of the Marquis of Hartington, a local MP who had been invited to preside at the inauguration. Darwen had grown rapidly in recent years from a small hamlet to a sizeable town of 30,000 inhabitants. Blackburn's market attracted traders away from Darwen and the Local Board was determined to see that revenue was kept at home. Charles Bell of London was commissioned as architect to the project and the Mayor, Alderman William Snape, laid the foundation stone on 2 October, 1880. The revised opening ceremony was held on 21 June, 1882, with Frederick Grafton MP officiating. Streamers and bunting festooned the building and dignitaries arrived in a fleet of horse drawn carriages to join in the celebrations. The market opened for business on 11 July and continued to be an important trading centre from then onwards. There have been some changes, as when the glass arcade was demolished in 1969 and a new covered market was built in 1975, but the main section continues to serve the community.

Above: Mohandas Gandhi (1869-1948), more generally known as Mahatma, was born in the Indian state of Gujarat. He came to London in 1888 to study law. In the 1890s he was active in South Africa, railing against the oppression and racism directed at Indians living there and helping found civil rights movements in that country. He returned to India in 1915 and involved himself during the interwar years in the struggle for Indian independence. Non co-operation and peaceful resistance were the weapons that he used. He visited Darwen in 1931 as part of a tour of Britain when he was campaigning for the rights of his people back home. He was invited to Lancashire to see how the local cotton industry had suffered because of the increase in tariffs levied on exports to India. Gandhi smiled serenely, as was his wont, but offered little in the way of help by action or deed. He pointed out the poverty in his homeland, but was non committal about anything else. His practice of dressing very simply and traditionally was meant to convey humility, but others saw it as a cynical ploy to gain attention and sympathy. Opinion was divided, but this group of women seem impressed. It is ironic that he was murdered the year after India became independent from British rule. Love him or loathe him, he was an iconic figure in the first half of the last century.

Below: 'Wings for Victory' Week was a fund raising scheme to encourage civilians to save their money in Government accounts, such as War Bonds, Savings Bonds, Defence Bonds and Savings Certificates. Cash would be paid into post offices or banks. In much the same way as War Weapons Week, it would coincide with a week of parades, exhibitions and other war paraphernalia. The No 1 Mobile Company, Home Guard, proudly marched past the General Post Office on Darwen Street to publicise the week and to display its determination to serve the country in its time of greatest need. Originally called the Land Army, the Home Guard was made up largely of volunteers who were too old or unfit to fight in the main armed services. Although never required to help rebuff an invasion, its members performed noble duties relieving regular troops of some more mundane jobs and provided good backup to civil defence units. In this particular week in 1943 it was decided that the national scheme would be themed around raising funds to purchase more bombers for the nation to take the fight to the enemy homeland. Although bombing cities was cruel and a dreadful thing to visit upon civilians, the decision has to be seen within the framework of life as it was in wartime. We can moralise now, but we do not have to live through an almost nightly blitz that killed tens of thousands of innocent folk. Back then, it was seen as payback time and a way to shorten the duration of a bloody war.

Above: Her Majesty Queen Elizabeth II inspected a guard of honour on King William Street during the royal visit of 1955. It had only been two years since her coronation and she was still a young monarch, not yet out of her 20s. Yet, she was the head of state over a Commonwealth of dozens of countries and millions of inhabitants. With her accession to the throne, we at home looked towards the future with optimism for what we hoped would be a new Elizabethan age. We had suffered badly during the war and the immediate postwar years were little better in economic terms. Rationing lasted until 1954 and the ordinary man in the street was still feeling the pinch. Consumer goods that we take for granted today were well out of his financial reach. Refrigerators, washing machines and televisions in our homes were luxury goods. A family car on the driveway was something for the middle classes. The austerity of the period was only just about to be cast aside. Those overseas countries that knuckled their foreheads in deference to our control began to show signs of unrest and pressed for change. We had already kissed goodbye to India and Ceylon and now it was the turn of Malaya and the African nations to flex their muscles as they sought autonomy.

The parties on the cobbles at Duke Street, Colne and Maudsley Street, Blackburn were just like thousands of similar ones held up and down the country on or around 2 June 1953, the day when Queen Elizabeth II was crowned in Westminster Abbey. Coronation Day was a drab affair in terms of the weather, but the occasion was a bright, revellous affair. The showers did not dampen our spirits, even if it made the fairy cakes and potted meat sandwiches go a little soggy and the orange squash became even more diluted. The church hall had been raided for trestle tables and mums had slaved away over hot ovens to make the day that bit special. Fancy dress

competitions were held and patriotic songs sung, rivalling the joyful scenes that were witnessed on VE Day at the end of the war. Union flags were hung from windowsills and jolly bunting draped from lampposts across the street as impromptu congas were danced on the pavement. The children thought the adults had gone mad, but that was not going to distract them from tucking into the goodies that lay on the tablecloths in front of them. The few who owned television sets suddenly found themselves very popular as neighbours crowded into their front rooms to watch the ceremonies being relayed from the capital.

Mercer Hall in Great Harwood was formally decorated for the occasion, with pictures of the Queen and her husband. 'Long may she reign' was quite a prophetic statement as Her Majesty's tenure on the throne is already one of the longest this country has ever seen. She will pass her great-great grandmother's record of over 63 years in 2015. In 1913, money was left in the will of Mary Mercer, the daughter of a wealthy factory owner, for the building of a community hall. Because of the first world war effort, it was not completed until 1921. Many events, including grand balls, were held in the interwar years. It was converted into a swimming baths in 1967.

Above: It will not surprise the reader to learn that Darwen's Edward Street won a prize for its decorations when the residents marked the occasion of Queen Elizabeth's Coronation Day on 2 June 1953. They had certainly pulled out all the stops and worked together as a tight little community to show that even the poorer sections of town knew how to put on a show. The people in the terraced housing were not just neighbours, they were also friends and confidantes. One family's troubles were someone else's to share and with which to help. Children called the parents of their playmates 'aunty' or 'uncle', even though there was no family link. Sometimes it was a problem that everyone knew everyone else's business, but that was a small price to pay for the friendships that were forged. The houses may have been humble, but they were home to many good, caring families. At one time they had outdoor lavvies with bits of newspaper hanging off a nail inside. A trip into the backyard on a freezing January evening was not an expedition to be undertaken lightly, especially if you tripped over the tin bath out there. There were doorsteps to be donkeystoned and front rooms that could be seen from the pavement to be kept spotless. When the houses were demolished to redevelop the area, more than just bricks and mortar were lost.

Right: This pageant to celebrate the Coronation in 1953 was one that had taken proud mums hours of dedication to help set up. Let us face facts, because you could not expect the men to lend a hand with anything that involved imagination and artistry. They were happy to celebrate the grand occasion with a bottle of Dutton's pale ale poured into a coronation mug. So, it was good old mum to the rescue. With a little bit of that make do and mend spirit and experience from the war, it was amazing what could be achieved with spare bits of material that were in the house somewhere. It was a crime to buy anything ready made unless you really had to, so out came the sewing machine and it was treadled away at top speed. Sons were pressed into action as page boys, often against their will. The same could not be said for their sisters. They just loved to dress up as little princesses and, for one of them, there was the special prize of being carnival queen. She looked very fetching in her elegant gown and regal crown. There might have been a twinge of jealousy felt be her attendants, but that was understandable. Anyway, it did not last long as they could all sense a feeling of togetherness as they shouted 'Hurrah!' for the real Queen.

Above: Perhaps this zany group was some sort of forerunner to the Bonzo Dog Doodah Band or the Temperance Seven. Maybe their inspiration came from Sid Millward and the Nitwits, but whatever the truth of the matter, we can be sure that they were fun to watch and listen to. The ensemble was part of the celebrations for Blackburn's centenary in 1951. It was a jolly time and, goodness knows, there had been too few of those since the VE and VJ parties in 1945. Six years of an austere Labour government that had nationalised everything that it could get its hands on, rationing that worsened after the war rather than easing and an economy in tatters as we went cap in hand to the Americans were more than enough. No wonder that these musicians blew off a little steam. The woman in the centre probably did not realise that her instrument was to become a major part of a music revolution in the 1950s. Eventually, we got rock and roll, but before it took over there was a craze for skiffle. It was developed here as a sort of English rockabilly music. The washboard and T chest bass augmented the guitars, banjo and drums that were used by small combos, The Vipers, Chas McDevitt, Shirley Douglas and Nancy Whiskey all had some success, though it was Lonnie Donegan who would be the daddy of all skiffle players.

Above and below: Local government buildings, the town centre and other distinctive parts of the borough were expensively dressed in honour of the Queen when she made her visit to the area in 1955. Specially created banners and flags were hung out to show allegiance and respect. Support for the monarchy did not have to be grandiose to convey the same message of loyalty and affection. On Victoria Street, now just off Barbara Castle Way and close to where the shopping centre stands, residents of the humble terraced houses strung up bunting they had left over from the Coronation two years earlier. The children were provided with little Union flags on sticks and they waved them vigorously as the royal guests went by. They only caught a glimpse of Her Majesty, but it was enough for them to believe that the gloved hand lifted in the back of the limousine was a personal acknowledgement of their support. Dressed in school uniforms or as Brownies and Cubs, they cheered themselves hoarse. It was a great day to remember.

A royal visit was a very special occasion as the Queen was held in high regard. Television was only just beginning to be popular and most people only had occasional opportunities to see the monarch on screen, usually via newsreels at the cinema.

carried the ubiquitous handbag that would become the trademark of her political enemy Margaret Thatcher a decade later. Accompanied by her personal detective, Mrs Castle was off to the Regency Hall where she was scheduled to open the Labour Party Fair. Born Barbara Betts in 1910, she hailed from Chesterfield, though spent her formative years in the West Riding. A bright child, she was head girl at Bradford Grammar School and became an Oxford University graduate. During this time she developed a passionate dislike of the elitism and sexism that pervaded academic and professional society of the 1930s. She soon became an official political activist, being elected to St Pancras Council while still in her 20s. She married Ted Castle in 1944 and threw her cap into the national ring by standing for Parliament in Blackburn in 1945. She became our MP in the Labour landslide and continued in that role until 1979 when she left Westminster to become a Member of the European Parliament. She was made a life peer in her own right in 1990 as Baroness Castle of Blackburn. Retirement meant little to her and she continued to be active right up to the end. At the age of 91, she lambasted the Chancellor, Gordon Brown, at the Labour Party Conference over pension policy. She died in 2002.

Above: There have been numerous road safety campaigns over the years. Back in the 1930s, Britain had just about the worst record in Europe for accidents and fatalities. It was little wonder that the government of the day brought in pedestrian crossings, cats' eyes, driving tests and that instructive booklet, the Highway Code. After the war, children became the focus of the road safety message. A cycling proficiency scheme was founded and special efforts made through the Stop, Look and Listen campaign. The Tufty Club was formed in 1961 and, within 12 months, had 60,000 youngsters enrolled. This grew to 2 million by 1972. The little squirrel's message to youngsters was explicit: take great care on the roads and pavements and learn how to cross roads safely and ride bicycles with responsibility. Schools played their part and included lessons on road safety in the curriculum. Crossing wardens or 'lollipop ladies' were employed to help out at the start and end of the school day. Here, Barbara Castle demonstrates her support for safer streets during a visit to Shadsworth High School. She was Minister for Transport at the time, a cabinet post she held from late 1965 to April 1968.

Right: Seen scurrying along a rain sodden pavement in the late 1960s, a smartly turned out Barbara Castle MP

LEISURE & PASTIMES

Nearly every soccer team has its ups and downs. There are periods of success when cups are won and championship trophies lifted. Then there are the other seasons when little goes right and relegation looms, followed by time spent in the doldrums before happier days return. Despite being a small town club, Blackburn Rovers has tasted life at the highest level in more than one era. The likes of Oldham and Barnsley have flickered briefly in recent years, but have slipped back into obscurity all too quickly. Our club continues to defy the odds and can reflect proudly on a heritage of professional football stretching back over 120 years when

Rovers was one of the 12 founding members of the Football League. The club was actually formed in 1875 following a meeting at the St Leger Hotel, King William Street, when two old boys of Shrewsbury School convened a get together for those interested in forming a team. The first games were played at Oozehead and, later, Leamington Street. It was from this latter base that the love affair with the FA Cup began. The famous trophy was lifted three times during the 1880s. Two years after entering the Football League a move to Ewood Park was made. The photograph of a full car park off Bolton Road was taken in the 1920s. By then we had won the Cup twice more in the 1890s and raced away with the league title in 1912 and 1914.

Blackburn was a name to be feared and another visit to the FA Cup Final was paid in 1928. By now Wembley was the venue and, despite the rain soaked pitch, the players were happy to wait and shake a royal hand before getting down to business. Huddersfield Town provided the opposition. The Yorkshire side was then one of the finest in the land, having won the league title three years running in the mid 1920s. However, we had beaten the much fancied Arsenal in the semi final and the fans were in a buoyant mood as kick off time approached. The Tykes were well beaten and the 3-1 scoreline meant a triumphant homecoming for our lads. A crowd the size of the one at Wembley turned out to cheer the side when the FA Cup was

Blackburn Rovers in Budapest (Rovers players wearing light shirts). The period was just before the 1914-1918 war and it was a great one for the Rovers. They were Football League champions twice in three years and probably just about the best known club in English soccer. They were one of the pioneers in continental tours, and certainly went to Belgium and Germany in 1910 and to Austria and Hungary the following summer. Players who went on tour included: Ashcroft, Crompton, Suttie, Walmsley, Stevenson, Ferguson, Bradshaw, Garbutt, Latheron, Aitkenhead, Cameron, Davis, Orr, and Anthony.

paraded in front of the Town Hall. Further success was not forthcoming in the 1930s and Rovers had a short spell in the second division.

After the last war sorry times returned as the team was relegated again and it took a decade until Blackburn was back in the top flight at the end of the 1957-58 season. By now such names as Bryan Douglas, Roy Vernon, Ronnie Clayton and Peter Dobing were known nationally and a new golden era began. Wembley beckoned again in 1960, but we lost to a strong Wolverhampton Wanderers team. Our cause was hindered by a serious injury to Dave Whelan, now the source of the money behind Wigan Athletic. Despite this setback, Rovers was now re-established as a major attraction. Yet, to most people's surprise, this status was shortlived. In 1966, the club suffered relegation from Division One and, in the 1970s, even slipped further into Division Three. The team photograph from the early 1970s shows one man who stuck with us through thick and thin. Derek Fazackerley, the stocky young man with long hair in the middle of the back row, made nearly 600 appearances for us in the years 1969-87.

The dressing room scene from c1970, possibly before a testimonial game, includes Keith Newton, Mike England and ex-player Ronnie Clayton, along with stars from other clubs, Denis Law, Pat Jennings, Geoff Hurst and Bobby Moore.

Blackburn Rovers became one of the founder members of the Premier League in 1992 and, with a little help from Jack Walker's millions, won the title in 1995, but we returned to our old ways when being relegated in 1999, before bouncing back again two years later.

Back: T Garbett, G Farrell, D Fazackerley. J Barton, B Conlon, F Goodwin
Front: B Wilson, T Shanahan, J Price, B Arentoft, G McDonald, M Heaton

Above: In 1960, Norman Wisdom had been a movie star for nearly a decade. He came into comedy after the last war, having served in the Army for 15 years. Initially a straight man for the magician David Nixon, he soon developed his own routine. His first film, 'Trouble in Store', was made in 1953. He was a major box office attraction for the next dozen years, before his star waned, though he still retained a degree of popularity that kept him busy throughout the rest of the last century and into this one. Rather bizarrely, Norman became a cult figure in Albania. The little king of slapstick came to Darwen when the Theatre Royal was disguised as a hotel for one of his films. 'There Was a Crooked Man' told of a law-abiding demolition expert duped by a gang of criminals into helping them. Needless to say, he is caught and jailed. When he is released he goes straight and then notices a leading citizen in his town is cheating his neighbours. Norman to the rescue! It was Wisdom's pulling power that meant several big names in the British movie world were happy to play second fiddle to him. This one had Andrew Cruickshank, Alfred Marks and Susannah York in the supporting cast.

Right: Just be very careful because that swan can hurt. If it thinks that there is any danger to its young, then watch out. The beak can provide the unwary with a very painful nip and the powerful wings are quite capable of breaking a child's arm as easily as you might snap a matchstick. The swan is a noble creature, but she holds no truck with those wanting to invade her privacy. However, if you are the provider of a few tasty morsels, then that is all right. With good reason, the children enjoying their time at Queen's Park were being watchful as they tore up the bread they were feeding to the birds. Our Victorian ancestors were very keen on providing open spaces in which the working classes could roam. Perhaps the wealthy benefactors who provided such amenities saw it as a way to ease their consciences. Many of them were factory and mill owners and employed people who worked in unhealthy and dangerous conditions. The park was once part of the Audley Hall estate and was opened in 1887 at a cost of £10,000 to mark Queen Victoria's golden jubilee. The lake was opened in 1888. It is now the park's main feature with two sections linked by a narrow channel and sourced by Audley Brook.

Right: The local neighbourhood watch members and the police force held a joint sports day in Barnoldswick as a community exercise. WPC Clayton posed with this group of youngsters who enjoyed being the centre of attention. No doubt the equal opportunities people will have something to say about the fact that it is the little lads who are sitting in the Panda car, but the photographer could only record what was happening without being too worried about political correctness. The girl leaning on the door will have long been a mother by now. Do you think that she might have told her own daughter in later years that wasting good money on face painting was a silly use of resources? If so, let us hope that this picture is sent to her.

Above: The New Inn on Victoria Street in the 1950s. It was demolished to make way for the Littlewoods stores, the New Inn formerly stood on the corner of Church Street, and there was a passage in the rear indicating where the sweating coach horses were to be fed and watered in the inn yard. Its coaching activities were in full swing in 1824, when the independent Post Coach arrived every day from Manchester at 2 p.m. and left shortly after for Preston and Lancaster.

Below: Looking along Ainsworth Street from Victoria Street some 60 years ago, a group of mums paused for a gossip outside one of the town's old watering holes. The Golden Lion was a popular place for a tipple in the days when pubs had smoking rooms, vaults and lounge bars. There a man could enjoy a Woodbine along with a game of dominoes, fives and threes, don, cribbage or darts on a log end. Calls such as 'ten for game', 'pegging out', 'Morgan's orchard' or 'two in a bed' were all part and parcel of the language of these pastimes. The mothers passing the time of day on the pavement would never have dreamed of bringing the little ones inside the pub doors. Yet, some modern hostelries have signs up asking parents to take home their offspring at 8.30 pm.

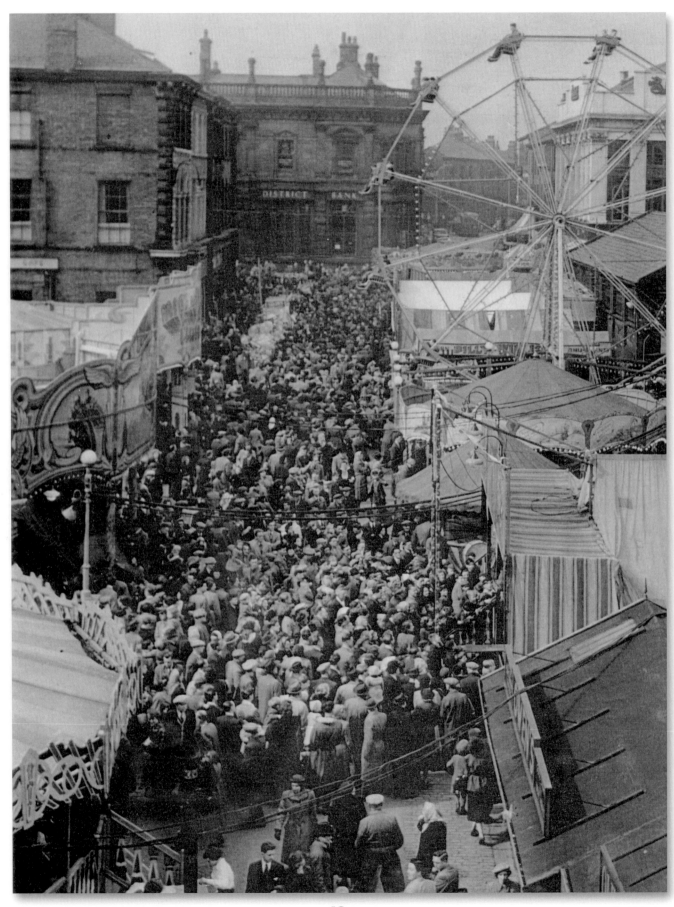

Left: 'The fair's here!' How those words transformed the prospect of a visit to town, no longer a dreary chore following your parents round as they did their weekend shopping. Even if it wasn't open yet, even if the stalls were still being set up, the rides assembled, even if you couldn't go till Easter Day, just it being there, just a glimpse of the bright wagons and exciting paraphernalia in dull old Market Square brought excitement, new horizons, a touch of the exotic. And when you did go at last, when it was all up and running, when the generators were chugging and the music was reverberating, when the smells of fried onions were vying with the scent of candy floss - what wonders, what adventures, what magic. There was so much – the rides, sedate horses for the young ones; the dodgems; the waltzer for the teenagers, a blur of girls' faces distorted by screams; the helter-skelter; the wheel with its human cargo, legs dangling, silhouetted against the sky, and then all the stalls.

There were those with rows of goldfish bowls and if you could get a ping-pong ball in one, you'd win a gold-fish in a plastic bag. There was hoop-la and the coconut shy. There was one with plastic ducks, hook one and it would have a number underneath which corresponded to a prize, never alas one of the train sets or gorgeous dolls on display, but a chalk ornament, or a packet of sweets. There were rifle ranges where demobbed soldiers would aim at ping-pong balls dancing on jets of water, and the less ambitious would shoot at tin men. Three down and you got a prize – the ubiquitous chalk ornament, more likely than not.

There were amusement arcades with penny in the slot machines and those with cranes suspended over an array of prizes: soft toys, watches, jewellery, a 10 bob note in a plastic tube. You could manoeuvre the crane over the chosen prize, lower it and make a grab. Sometimes a precious gift would be secured and you'd inch the crane towards the chute that would deposit it into your hands, but always; always, the gift slipped from the crane's grasp at the last minute. There were stalls selling toffee apples, brandy snap, candy floss. There were stalls selling hamburgers, hot dogs and chips. There were stalls selling ice cream and milk shakes and pop. You could buy sweets, novelties made out of rock, pop corn, slabs of toffee. You could buy toys – red Indian outfits, cowboy outfits, bows and arrows, pop-guns, all guaranteed to last until the fair had left town. And then your parents would say it was time to go, or that they were spent up. And as the sky was growing darker the crowds leaving would be replaced by older teenagers arriving, young men with quiffs and drain-pipe trousers, young women with beehive hair dos and white stilettos. There would be a hint of glamour and danger in the air.The sounds of the fair would fade as you climbed up the hill out of town. Next day or the day after it would be gone and Market Square would be as dull as ever – until the next time!

Above: Is that a 'Bald Eagle' on the Rt Honourable Lady Thatchers' shoulder? Jim Smith, nicknamed The Bald Eagle, is seen here introducing Tony Parks and his fellow players to Lady Thatcher MP in 1977. The highlight of the visit was when she was made honoury Life President of Blackburn Rovers AFC.

Smith moved into football management at Boston and after a good start he was offered the job at Colchester United FC in November 1972. Success came quickly as Smith guided them to the Football League Fourth Division title in 1974. His performance at the club attracted the attention of bigger clubs, and in 1975 he quit the club, and hung up his boots, to join Blackburn Rovers as manager. He led Blackburn for three years before leaving to be appointed boss of Birmingham City in 1978.

Crown Paints - Brushstrokes of History

With a story spanning three centuries, Crown Paints Limited, based in Darwen, near Blackburn, has a rich pedigree in 'decorative coatings', with its leading brands today including Crown, Sadolin, Sandtex, Macpherson Permoglaze and Berger. In 2008 a management buy out returned the business to British ownership and ensured its future independence.

With its headquarters in Darwen, Crown Paints has annual revenue in excess of £180 million across the UK and Ireland (with a further small export business). The company employs 1,500 people and operates two manufacturing sites, one in Darwen and another in Hull, together with strategic warehouse depots located in Warrington, Dublin and Belfast. The business also has an extensive network of Crown Decorator Centres across the UK and Ireland.

The Crown Paints story began in Darwen in 1777 when one James Greenway came to the town from Oxfordshire. He built the Dob Meadows Print Shop for printing calico, situated at the bottom of Sunnyhurst Woods. There is still a Greenway Street as a reminder of his name.

The story then moves to the Potter family. John Potter was a businessman from Manchester (and the uncle of Beatrix Potter). He met Sarah Greenway, the daughter of James Greenway, fell in love, and moved to Darwen to marry her. They lived at Churchbank.

*Above left: Early Walpamur water paint. **Above:** Queens Mill, a branch of the 'Potters' activities famous for manufacturing Anaglypta and Lincrusta relief decorations. When Akzo Nobel sold relief to Crown Wallcoverings in 2001 production moved and Queens Mill was used as a paint warehouse. **Below:** Walpamur shop and van.*

As a memorial John Charles Potter gave the Potters Lych Gate entry to Sunnyhurst Woods - a gift in memory of the time the Potters lived in Darwen. John Guy Potter stood unsuccessfully in parliamentary elections for the Liberal Party several times. He was the acquaintance of members of parliament in Manchester, and when Potters' workers required new housing it is likely that he had influence over the naming of the roads, giving rise to Cobden Street and Bright Street amongst others. The last family member with links to paint and wallpaper was J.J.G. Mellor, a great grandson of Charles Potter. Mellor was the director of Walpamur paints from 1922 to 1947.

John Potter became a partner in James Greenway's calico printing business which took over the Bury Fold Print Shop in 1821 where John worked until 1835. John and Sarah Potter had nine children including Charles, Harold and Edwin. John Potter was buried at Holy Trinity Church, later renamed St Peter's.

The story continued with John's son, Charles Potter, who was taken into partnership in his father's business. However, during the mid-1830s Charles was interested in the experiments taking place in Tamworth and Liverpool to see if wallpaper could be printed mechanically onto calico. Charles was well placed to try his hand at this new innovation with paper making being a major part of industry in Darwen. Charles adapted a calico printing machine for printing paper and his brother Harold patented it in 1839. The earliest machine printed using only four colours; later ones had twenty. The design of the wallpaper was engraved on metal rollers.

In order to make full use of the machine Charles Potter needed somewhere to work. Fortunately, his brother Edwin had built Belgrave Mill in 1836 and by 1840 they were commercially producing wallpaper at Belgrave, under the trade name C. H and E. Potter. They later bought Hiltons Paper Mill (subsequently Darwen Paper Mill) for paper production.

In 1880 New Livesey Mill was built behind Belgrave. It was burned down in 1920 and was rebuilt in 1922. Both Belgrave Mill and Livesey Mill would be rebuilt several times over the years.

The Potter family would stay in Darwen, as directors of Wallpaper until 1903. John Guy Potter, Charles' son, joined his father as a partner in 1849, and his son, John Charles Potter, in turn joined him as a partner in 1884. They lived in Earnsdale House on Earnsdale Road (below Dingle house, where bungalows would eventually be built).

To enable their business to flourish the Potters took on several outside partners, many of whom became well known figures around Darwen. For example the Market Hall bears the name of one of the partners a William Snape. Who originally started at Potters wallpaper as a designer in 1846, eventually becoming a full partner in the business.

Above: research and new product development has been the lifeblood of Crown Paints since 1904 when Hollins Distemper water based paints were developed. **Left and below:** A newpaper article (left) and artists impression (below) of the proposed building of Crown House. Bottom: A 1950s aerial of the current Darwen site prior to the building of Crown House HQ Administration building in 1958.

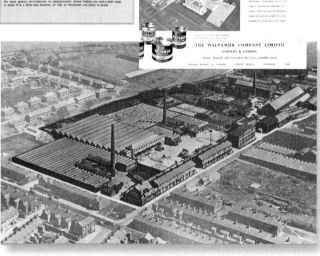

Following his retirement William Snape took a leading role in creating the Municipal Borough of Darwen and was elected its first Mayor in 1878, a position he held for three years. During this time he commissioned the building of the Market Hall, culverted the River Darwen to bring it out at Shorey Bank and then built the Technical College. Snape lived at Lynwood House and is recalled in the name Snape Road. He died in 1888 at Grange over Sands.

Often whole families worked with the Potters. Walmsley Preston, who lived at Falcon House (later the Liberal Club) was a partner of the Potters in the nineteenth century. His nephew, Walmsley Preston Kay, worked at Potters for 37 years and is remembered as the Mayor of Darwen who was responsible for commissioning the Tudor Kiosk in Sunnyhurst Woods.

Another prominent family were the Huntingtons. James Huntington, the eldest brother, came to work for Potters as a wallpaper designer. He was already well known in London, and his appointment was considered quite a coup at the time. In 1872 he bought Astley Bank – which would eventually become a hotel. The house was originally erected in the mid-1840s by the Kershaw-Smalley family. Both James, and his brother Charles Philip Huntington lived there. They extended both the land and the property. Nearby Huntington Road was named after the family. James Huntington died in 1878 and left funds for the workers in his will. In recognition of his influence and generosity a fountain known as the Huntington Fountain was built in Bold Venture Park. This was scrapped for its metal during the Second World War, though traces of it can still be seen.

The next brother, William Huntington, came to Darwen in 1874 as head of the commercial department. He lived at Orchard Bank (subsequently the Alexandra pub), which was built in 1855. In 1898 William set about forming the 'Wallpaper Manufacturers', which was a merger between all the wallpaper manufacturers in the area. Later William and his son Arthur encouraged the firm to go ahead with experiments in paint manufacturing. In 1878 William bought Woodlands (a house built by Thomas Ashton in 1864) which passed to Arthur on his death.

William Huntington was made a director of the Manchester and County Bank in 1895 and was the High Sheriff for Lancashire in 1898. He was the first Chairman of the old Technical School and

Above left: *It is hard to imagine a time before computers, yet here we see the girls in the general typing room in the 1950s processing letters and documents using manual typewriters. This function would be mirrored within most companies at this time.* ***Left:*** *Labelling, a labour of love, hand applying colour chips to the Walpamur water paints.* ***Below:*** *A corner of the packing department showing the labour intensive production process.*

laid the foundation stone of the Conservative Club. He died in 1911 leaving £2,000 in trust for regular public lectures; he also he left money to the workers of the Wallpaper Manufacturers, who as a tribute to him put up the Huntington Bridge in Sunnyhurst Woods in 1912.

Charles Huntington was made a Justice of the Peace in 1878, and in 1892 he became the MP for Darwen for the Liberal Party. He introduced electricity to the Potters factory in 1881. In 1898 he became Mayor of Darwen, and saw the erection of Darwen Tower. On June 28, 1906, he was made a Baronet, but lived only six months longer and died in January 1907.

During these years the company showed remarkable growth. It built, bought and amalgamated with many of the mills around Darwen including Sunnybank Mill, bought by Potters in 1858, and Woodfold Mill built by William Snape in 1885 for his son Gerald to work as a cotton manufacturer. Livesey Fold Print Works were in turn owned by James Greenway, the Potters and William Snape; a product called 'sanitary paper' was produced here before production was moved to nearby Orchard Mill. The site was later occupied and extensively redeveloped by ICI but some of the original building can still be seen.

From early on, Potters focussed on developing distribution centres around the country, and indeed around the world. Within Darwen there were two official centres to buy Crown wallpaper and paint in the twentieth century. The first one, which was advertised in Barretts directory of

1898, was at 7 Church Street. A more recent one was Yates' on Duckworth Road, which was trading until the mid-1990s.

The original engraving works where the wallpaper printing rollers were embossed can be seen on Almond Street. Initially it was used simply to store rollers then, in 1946, it was taken over by Belgrave Mill to make the rollers. On Ashworth Street there can still be seen the Belgrave works fire station of 1908.

A large investment for Potters was the acquisition of Hollins Mill. This was originally Hollins Bleach works, built in 1832 by Robert Turner, a calico

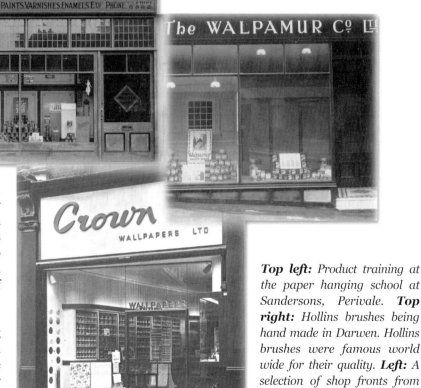

Top left: Product training at the paper hanging school at Sandersons, Perivale. Top right: Hollins brushes being hand made in Darwen. Hollins brushes were famous world wide for their quality. Left: A selection of shop fronts from times past .

maker (who used the river to provide power via a 22 ft waterwheel). It was sold in 1843 by William Turner (Robert's son) to Potters, who turned it into their main paper making site. By the 1870s it had four machines for making wallpaper base, newsprint and other papers. They put up Queens Mill in 1894 to produce Anaglypta, for which Potters had recently acquired

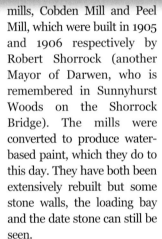

the rights. The mill underwent major reconstruction in the late 1920s with the installation of new machinery and further rebuilding from 1950 - 54. It ceased to be used early this century and has since been knocked down.

In 1904, in a shed adjoining Hollins paper mills, the first steps into water-based paint production began, and by 1906 Hollins Distemper was produced. Its success was such that by 1910 salesmen were being employed to sell the paint and the new company was named Walpamur (taking the initials from Wallpaper Manufacturers). Its first logo depicted Jubilee Tower, India Mill, Hollins Paper Mill and St John's Church steeple in Darwen.

The Walpamur company grew throughout the 1920s and in the early 1930s it bought the neighbouring textile mills, Cobden Mill and Peel Mill, which were built in 1905 and 1906 respectively by Robert Shorrock (another Mayor of Darwen, who is remembered in Sunnyhurst Woods on the Shorrock Bridge). The mills were converted to produce water-based paint, which they do to this day. They have both been extensively rebuilt but some stone walls, the loading bay and the date stone can still be seen.

During the First World War paint production at the site focused on providing varnish for bullets being sent to France, a necessary step to prolong their useful life. During the Second World War paint was produced for blackouts, reflective paint for the roads, and large quantities of paint was made for planes. Indeed all the planes taking part in the D-day landings had been painted with Walpamur, a fact commended by the Ministry of Defence. Slight changes to the printing machines also enabled the company to prepare fittings for the metal canisters used for carrying bomb fuses. Much of this work was carried out by women "whose deft fingers" (according to the book 'Wallpapers and War') "were just suited to do the work, and they entered into it with zest".

Top: The workers of Crown paints have always enjoyed a social side to their job. Here pensioners from Walpamur line up by the coaches ready for their day trip. ***Above left:*** Crowds gather outside to catch a glimpse of the Queen on her visit to Walpamur in 1968. ***Left:*** The Queen talking to Tom Graham, with (left) Fred Lewis, Sam Dix and Charles Alpe.

By the time of the Queen's visit the company had been taken over by Reed International, and was linked by name with Crown wallpaper. After this various company name changes took place; William Holdings in the 1980s, then Berger Paints which changed the name to Crown Berger. In 1990 it was taken over by Nobel Industries, which then joined with Akzo to become Akzo Nobel in 1994, a Dutch multi-national chemicals business.

The Belgrave site, which had been extensively rebuilt in the 1950s, closed in 2003 due to a decline in the wallpaper market after 157 years of business. In 2008 Akzo Nobel acquired ICI Worldwide and divested Crown Paints UK and Ireland jointly to its management team and the investment company Endless LLP.

After the Second World War business was going well at Walpamur. In 1949 the firm was granted a Royal Warrant as suppliers to King George VI, a warrant subsequently renewed by Queen Elizabeth II.

Crown Paints Ltd now became once again a truly independent business.

Top left: Throughout the Crown Paints history training their staff and customers on the use of its products has been an important function. Pictured is John Prior, Trade Training Manager, advising a decorator on the virtues of Permoglaze gloss. Left: A selection of Crown Paints including Rovers Blue

In 1958 Crown House, the administrative offices, was built; and in 1963 a private power station was erected above Hollins Mill, which was used until Darwen Paper Mill closed, making it uneconomical.

made especially to celebrate the club sponsorship of Blackburn Rovers in 2008. Bottom left: The entrance to Crown House. Left and below: Interior and exterior views of a Crown Decorating Trade Centre.

Her Majesty Queen Elizabeth II visited the Darwen Walpamur head office site off Hollins Road in 1968. This was a proud day for the company and helped put Darwen on the map.

In 1910, the electric tram was part of a growth industry inside the public transport system. Car after car stretched the length of the depot as around a couple of dozen employees posed for this photograph. Those with the cloth caps or overalls can be firmly placed in the 'get your hands dirty' brigade. Rather quaintly, Parliament had blocked the municipal owning of tram companies for much of the previous century. There were any number of private organisations operating horse drawn vehicles on their own tracks, but it was not until the passing of the Tramways Act of 1870 that local authorities were permitted to build the lines. Even then, they had to lease out the running of the businesses to private companies for a further decade until a new Act of Parliament was passed. The ostentatiously named Blackburn and Over Darwen Tram Company was the main operator in and around Blackburn, but it ran foul of the law on a number of occasions with its practice of frequent overloading and poor safety record. In 1898 the two town corporations purchased the company and divided the track and rolling stock between them. Darwen electrified its part of the system in 1901 and Blackburn followed suit a little later. The latter's tramway bye-laws included some regulations that might be of interest today. Passengers were forbidden to use obscene language, smoke or carry firearms.

TRANSPORT

Below: The tram photographed at Sudell Cross was one of the early open topped ones that plied their trade in the early 1900s. They made the town centre more accessible to those living in the outlying districts and helped improve their lives and the amount of business conducted by the retail outlets as their client base expanded. It was an interesting time of change. Tragically, for many of the young men and older boys in the photograph, the world was changing as well. The international influence of the British Empire was under threat as other European nations flexed their political and military muscles.

Top right: 'Long live the King' was the motto on the front of this gaily decorated tram. The driver and conductor posed with the official in the straw boater in this tribute to the Coronation celebrations for King Edward VII. He had waited in the wings for nearly 60 years. Perhaps our present Prince of Wales will pass that record in 2012, but at this moment Prince Albert Edward was the longest serving heir apparent that this country had ever seen. He assumed the throne in January 1901 and his coronation took place on 9 August, 1902. Not many people in the country could recall clearly his mother's accession to the throne. After all, it was back in 1837 when Victoria was crowned. After her husband's death in 1861, the Queen spent much of her time away from the public gaze. Albert Edward represented his mother at many official functions during his time in waiting. He was a restless spirit and found life as a king in the distant future too boring in the present. He developed a reputation as a playboy and was

involved in countless scandals with women from all walks of life. Despite all these failings, he was feted when his Coronation Day came along. The tram in the picture is a Darwen open top car that had pulled up outside Westwood in Hollins Grove. The building later became a care home for the elderly.

Below: Devastation in Darwen on 20th September 1926. The number 11 Corporation tram was making the first journey of the day from Hoddlesden to Darwen when it ran out of control on the steep decent down Sudell Road. The tram failed to take the sharp bend at the bottom of the hill and crashed into the billiard hall in Bridge Street. One man was killed and another died of his injuries the following day. Another seven were hurt including the driver and conductor. On theory at the time, was that lightening may have affected the overhead trolley wire.

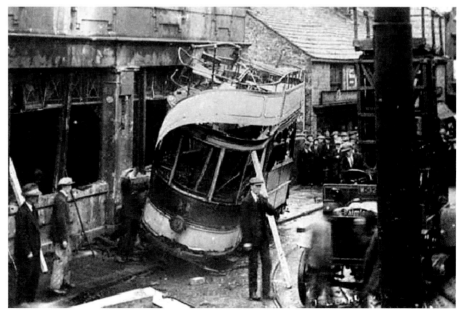

riding the carriages, because the three classes of travel had facilities of differing levels of comfort and they were priced accordingly. But departure and destination points were just the same, even if fraternisation between the differing strata was avoided. The cabs and carriages brought the more well to do from their homes on the outskirts of town, while the lesser fry caught the recently introduced tram or simply walked to the station from their terraced housing. In the foreground, the long, flowing dresses of the Edwardian ladies were part of the uniform of people who had both style and the money with which to support it. The young beaux with their straw boaters and canes stayed aloof from the scruffy working classes in their flat caps in what was very much a 'them and us' society. The first chinks in that way of thinking would come on the battlefields of Europe in a few years' time when machine gun bullets did not differentiate between the haves and have nots.

Above: The concourse at the front of Blackburn Station was a busy place, as we can see in this view taken in the first few years of the last century. Rail travel was, in one way, a great social leveller. People from all walks of life could avail themselves of the main form of public transport that had become immensely popular over the preceding half century. There was still a social and economic division when actually

Below: Seen in 1970, this family was making its way towards the main entrance to the railway station. By then, travelling by train was an experience that people had enjoyed for over a century. Steam locomotives came to Blackburn in the 1840s. At first, as with the rest of the country, there were a number of companies with their own lines and interests who were all in competition with one another. In this part of Lancashire, the Blackburn and Preston Railway (BPR) had a major rival in the organisation that went under the unwieldy name of the Bolton, Blackburn, Clitheroe and West Yorkshire Railway. Not surprisingly, it was more commonly referred to as the 'Bolton Company'. At first, the two groups shared the BPR station at Stoneybutts, later the Boulevard. However, competitors do not make easy bedfellows and disagreements soon surfaced over a variety of dealings and practices. The Bolton Company built its own station at Bolton Road and the BPR evolved into the East Lancashire Railway. Having parted company, the two got back together in 1857 to become part of the large Lancashire and Yorkshire Railway. By the time that this group of travellers was photographed, many more changes had been experienced and the railways were now well established nationally as British Rail.

Left: The Liverpool-Leeds canal in 1960 with now vanished Whitebirk power station in the background. The electricity plant opened by Blackburn Corporation as the Blackburn (East) Generating Station in 1921., originally had wooden cooling towers. Its four 250 ft reinforced concrete towers were erected between 1942 and 1954. The power station consumed vast tonnages of coal brought by canal from the Burnley coalfield. But the waterways were doomed as a commercial artery by the 13-week 'Big Freeze' winter of early 1963 which kept the canal ice-bound for so long that the transport of freight by barge in East Lanacashire never recovered. Generating ended at Whitebirk in 1976, although the cooling towers were not demolshed until 1983.

Blackburn's last tram left the Boulevard for the Intack depot shortly after 11.30pm on 3 September, 1949. Specially illuminated for the occasion, it was driven by Transport Commitee Chairman, Councillor Robert Weir, with the Mayor and Mayoress and council members and officials as passengers. At Intack, Councillor Weir was besieged by autograph hunters and, along the route, many people placed pennies on the tramlines - to be crushed as souvenirs. At the depot Mr Arthur Potts took over the helm for the honour of driving the last tram into the shed, having done the same to the town's last steam tram nearly fifty years before.

ROYAL VISITS

Below: Every dignitary who was something, and even a few who were not, was anxious to be seen close to the royal couple as they graced Blackburn with a visit on 10 July, 1913. You could dine out on the story for weeks to come. King George V and Queen Mary cut handsome figures as they left the Town Hall after an official reception. The House of Saxe-Coburg-Gotha, to which the King belonged, was not universally popular. Rumblings of revolution at home and abroad meant that the monarchy was less secure than it had been in earlier times. The rise in popularity of left wing political parties troubled the royal family and its government. The status quo of the ruling classes was under threat. Anarchists and dissidents made their views known both via the soapbox and more violent means. The Portuguese monarchy was overthrown in the 1910 revolt and gunfire was heard in the East End of London in 1911 during the siege of Sidney Street that saw an armed battle between police and protesters that left several dead on both sides. Relations between King George's cousin, the German Kaiser, and Britain were strained almost to breaking point. Another cousin, the Russian Tsar Nicholas, was facing unrest among his subjects. They would rise up four years later when the Tsar and his family were assassinated.

Right and bottom right: The leafy lanes leading to Roe Lee Mill were packed with wellwishers waiting to see the King and Queen as their stately progress took them slowly along the road to their destination. It was a proud day for these local residents as they knew that it was an honour for their town to able to fete such important people. Not everyone touched a forelock or bowed a head as the motorcade moved by. There were some who muttered about the Germanic influence in royal circles. We all knew about King George V's pedigree, but his wife, the former Mary of Teck, was not exactly Ramsbottom through and through. The papers were full of talk of the growth of German military might. The top naval officer, Admiral von Tirpitz, had

announced that 14 new warships had been commissioned. It was not just ordinary people who were edgy as the monarchy was also fully aware of its own vulnerability. Earlier in 1913, the King of Greece was assassinated and those at Buckingham Palace made sure that security was stepped up for the King and Queen on their travels. Even after war on Germany was declared the following year, there were some who doubted George and Mary's true allegiances. However, they did much to allay those suspicions in 1917 by renaming the family as the Windsors. Now, that was a proper English sounding name.

Above: Britain was now in the Edwardian era. It only lasted for a decade, but saw the birth or development of so many things that we now take for granted. The first motor cars were seen on the streets and the use of electricity became more widespread. The Wright brothers at Kitty Hawk made the first successful aeroplane flight and old age pensions were introduced. The Victorian age of gaslamps, steam and horse drawn road vehicles was to undergo a revolution. The gentry clung to some of the old ways for a time. On ceremonial occasions, they dressed in their finery, with the women donning long, flowing skirts and fancifully decorated hats, and the men in frock coats and toppers. They failed to espouse the use of any newfangled horseless carriage, but opted for the traditional sort, pulled by noble steeds whose blood was as blue as that of their passengers. On 30 September, 1905, Princess Louise came to call. As the eldest daughter of King Edward VII, she would be awarded the title of Princess Royal just six weeks after she came to Blackburn. Louise was married to the Earl of Fife. He died in 1912 after falling ill with pleurisy in Egypt as the couple recuperated from being shipwrecked off the Moroccan coast. She died in 1931, aged 63.

Above: The Duke of Kent had something of a dubious reputation as a roué and was followed by scandal throughout his earlier years. However, he seemed to settle down after his marriage and concentrated on supporting his brother, King George VI, by undertaking a number of official duties. His visit to Blackburn in 1938 was just one of those where he represented the monarch. Here he is seen leaving the Sunshine Club. This was an institution that looked after the needs of unemployed women, offering both succour and support. The man following the Duke appears to be a little hot under the collar. Whether he was perturbed by what he had just experienced or merely had an itch is not recorded. The club was just one of many ports of call that this member of the royal family made during a whistle stop tour of the town and its neighbourhood. The black Rolls-Royce that whisked him from place to place covered quite a few miles that day.

Below: The residents of Great Harwood gazed at the man in the centre of the group heading along their street. His world was so different from theirs. They had struggled through the interwar depression years, scrimping and saving, though with very little of the latter. It was difficult for them to make ends meet. Existence in the back to back terraced houses was a never ending round of worry about putting food on the table or clothes on their backs. Those marching down the road, like some forerunners of gunslingers in the movie 'High Noon', acted as if they owned the place. In a way, they did. They could buy and sell anyone in the vicinity, such was their privileged niche in society. Women in humble pinnies looked at the furs and trappings of the upper classes and knew that their lives were a million miles apart. The debonair chap carrying his homburg in his hand was the Duke of Kent. Pictured in 1938, he was born in 1902 as Prince George, the fourth son to King George V and Queen Mary. He married Princess Marina of Greece in 1934. They had three children, but the family was hit by tragedy in 1942 when the Duke perished in a plane crash in Scotland.

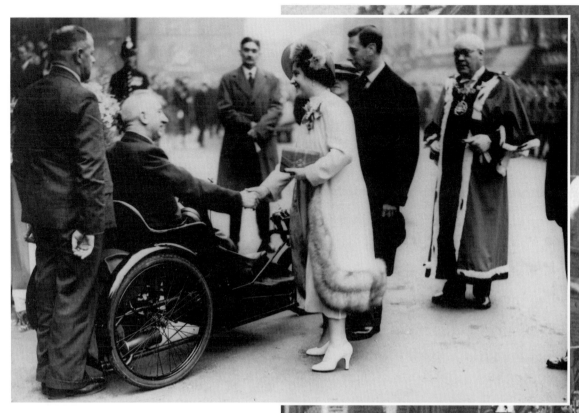

Above: King George VI and Queen Elizabeth came to Blackburn in June 1948. Those in invalid carriages, some of whom were war veterans, were given pride of place outside the Town Hall so that they could get the best view of their royal guests. Born Elizabeth Bowes-Lyons, in 1900, most readers will know this woman as the 'Queen Mum'. This affectionate soubriquet became hers in her later life as she slipped into the background after the death of her husband in 1952. The grand old lady lived to the remarkable age of 101, but she played a major role in royal circles either side of the last war. A firm reactionary, she was horrified when her brother-in-law abdicated in late 1936. For him to abandon his duties was bad enough, but it meant that her husband was pressed into service to assume a throne for which he was unprepared. The new king was a shy and diffident man who was afflicted with a stutter that worsened under stress. Like no consort before or since, Queen Elizabeth took the lead when out in public. Even here, she is the one doing the greeting and indulging in small talk. During the war she became the darling of the nation with her steadfast determination to stay within these shores when others would have run off to safety in some haven, such as Canada. It was the King who trailed in her wake, rather than vice versa.

A cavalcade of horses and carriages passed St George's Church, demolished in 1974, as a large crowd turned out to see the special visitors who had come to town. Only a royal visit could generate such fervour. The Prince and Princess of Wales, the future Edward VII and his consort Alexandra, were the main guests. They were accompanied by the Mayor and Mayoress, with the Marquis of Hartington also in attendance. The Marquis was born Spencer Cavendish and was heir to the Duke of Devonshire. The title he held at this time was merely honorary until he assumed the dukedom upon his father's death in 1891. At the time of this photograph, that dates from the 1880s, he was able to sit in the House of Commons as the town's MP because his title was not a peerage in its own right. This was quite a frequent occurrence in British politics at the time, ensuring that sons of members of the House of Lords sat in the other chamber. This helped preserve the elitism and influence of the ruling classes. Cavendish or Hartington had the distinction of leading three differently named political parties during his time at Westminster, namely the Liberals, the Liberal Unionists and the Unionists. He was an influential figure who was close to becoming prime minister on several occasions.

Above: If there was ever any doubt about the popularity of the monarchy in the mid 1950s, then this photograph of the scene outside the Town Hall on King William Street should allay any reservations. Thousands of onlookers were present, not just here, but along the whole route that the Queen and Prince Philip took on their way into the centre. A large regimental presence mounted a guard of honour and the standard was lowered in greeting as Queen Elizabeth stood to attention to accept this display of loyalty. The whole town had come to a standstill to pay homage to the woman who represented the future for which we all wished. She was young and vibrant and was able to look forward to the rest of the century with enthusiastic eyes towards a successful and rewarding life. Her subjects hoped for the same and that she would be the figurehead in our nation's recovery.

The population had spent a decade trying to recover from the privations of war and its aftermath. There was hope on the horizon, at last. The job market was healthy and the economy was showing signs of recovery. Britain was starting to stand on its own feet and become a major player in trade and international influence once more.

Top right: Just as it had been for the Coronation two years earlier, the town centre was festooned with garlands and banners in honour of the Queen and Prince Philip. To the right, a solitary police rider on horseback moved infront of the crowd. There was little need for the deployment of man or beast as bystanders knew how to behave. There was very little in the way of pushing and shoving. People stood in an orderly fashion and

there was no threat to anyone's safety, either in the crowd or among the gathered VIPs. Security was minimal. It would have been unheard of to consider a threat to the security of the crowned head of Britain and its Commonwealth. Sadly, all of that has changed in more recent years. Now, people in high office, and even those on some sort of celebrity 'A' list, feel vulnerable. Rash of attacks on such figures began with the assassination of President Kennedy in 1963.

difficult for them to take in everything that they see. In so many of the calls made to businesses, town halls, churches and schools those coming to tour must feel that they have seen it all before in some other town. Yet, the innate sense of good manners and upper crust breeding helps such as the Queen and Prince Philip to display interest even when there is very little.

Right: The limousines swished by Sudell Cross in the early spring of 1955. The police pilot car led the way, with the royal conveyance following closely behind. The location where this photograph was taken has seen a number of changes over the years as both the crossroads and the highway have been subject to alteration. A new feature, called 'The Braid', was unveiled here in 2007. Designed by Simon Watkinson, the illuminated feature cost over £1 million. The passengers in the cars were on their way to the cathedral, the Church of St Mary the Virgin. When the royal party visits any town it must be

Below: Any vantage point, however precarious, was claimed when Queen Elizabeth II and the Duke of Edinburgh visited Mullard's in 1955. The factory was a huge plant, covering 46 acres. It was famous for its high volume valve production. The company came to Blackburn in 1938 and, partly thanks to the wartime demand, was soon working flat out. As well as its trademark valves, aircraft components rolled off the production lines. A former Admiralty officer with experience in the lighting and communications fields, Stanley Mullard founded his own business in 1920 as the Mullard Radio Valve Company after working for the Z Electric Light Company. He took over the premises of his former employers and then built his own works in Hammersmith. The formation of the BBC in 1922 and the growth in home radio was an economic boon to him. Mullard collaborated with the Dutch giant, Philips, and sold out to them in 1927. He continued to act as managing director until 1930, before retiring to grow flowers as a way of life. In a short time he had become a wealthy man. The plant at Whitebirk, to the northeast of the town, moved into parts for television sets in the 1950s to augment its other business. Stanley Mullard died in 1979, aged 95, but the firm continued to bear his name until Philips dropped it in 1988.

Right: Prince Philip took a ride in a Land Rover when travelling from Witton Park to Pleasington Playing Fields. Accompanied by the Parks Committee chairman, Alderman John Stirrup, the Duke of Edinburgh was enjoying a tour of some of the open air facilities in and around the town. Looking very dapper in his smart suit and sporting a freshly laundered handkerchief in his top pocket, the Queen's consort offered himself for all the public to see. He is a man who has enjoyed outdoor pursuits and you can almost see him here mentally exchanging his current mode of transport for the four in hand carriage that he was fond of driving in competition. The Duke spent many hours following and participating in this sport and became one of the country's best exponents of this brand of equestrian sports. His wife has always been a keen horsewoman as well, so it was hardly surprising that their only daughter, Princess Anne, should follow in their footsteps. She was to triumph on the international stage as a top showjumper and was gifted enough to represent her country at the Olympic Games. Anne's daughter, Zara, followed in the family footsteps with achievements that rivalled those of her mother. Quite remarkably, both these women won BBC TV's Sports' Personality of the Year awards. Their dad and grandfather was suitably proud.

love, he enjoyed travelling by a variety of means. Here he was revelling in sitting at the controls of the Whirlwind helicopter on the grounds of Witton Park, an estate once owned by the Feilden family. Although helicopters had been in use earlier in the century, it was not until 1942 that they began to be mass produced, thanks to new designs created by Igor Sikorsky. Westland Aircraft was formed in 1915. It built machines that were used in the First World War and supplied Supermarine Spitfires to the RAF in World War II after the parent Spitfire plant in Southampton was bombed. After this war, Westland moved into helicopter production and developed the Whirlwind from the Sikorsky S-55. The company suffered an economic downturn in the 1970s and 1980s. Controversial

Above: The Duke of Edinburgh is very much a naval man. During World War II, he was on active service in battleships and cruisers, performing with sufficient distinction to be mentioned in despatches. Although the sea remained his first attempts to rescue Westland resulted in the resignation of defence Secretary Michael Heseltine in 1986. The former Westland site at Weston-super-Mare is now home to The Helicopter Museum.

Above: They snapped away with their little box Brownies using black and white film to record the joys of the royal visit in 1955. The anxious three day wait for the photographs to be developed at Timothy White's was part of the fun. Just how good would the snaps be or were they going to be a disappointing waste of time because they were taken into the sun? The senior citizens, or th'old 'uns as they were then known, had bagged the best places at the front. Rightly so, because this was when youth venerated experience and old age. It was only proper that they should be afforded the respect of the best seats in the house, even if they needed a warming wrap or two to keep out the cold. The children behind them kept up the sort of racket that only kids can make for what seemed like hours. That is something that has not changed over the years. Perhaps the most notable sight is the nun in the centre of the crowd. Mother Superior was not watching and she could let rip to her heart's content. She had not enjoyed herself so much since Sister Concepta passed a photograph of Errol Flynn round the convent.

Left: Just every so often you can let your guard slip. The Queen was in the company of two men for whom radio valves and television components meant a great deal. These items provided work for many Blackburn residents as Mullard's was one of the biggest employers in the town in 1955. The two suited men depended upon their workforce and the products they turned out for their own livelihood. Mr W Armistead, the manager of the Glass Division, explained the function of the machinery under the watchful eye of the director, Mr C

De Wit. Mr Armistead spoke enthusiastically about the process and explained what was happening in great detail. The Queen was supposed to display bright-eyed interest, but the camera caught her mood as, for once, she allowed her true feelings to be displayed on her countenance. Who can blame her? Here is a young woman in her late 20s and she is expected to be fascinated by the nuts and bolts of manufacturing.

Above: Just how many bouquets of flowers has the Queen received during her reign on the British throne? They must run into thousands by now. Each one is just as graciously received as if it were the first she had ever been given. After accepting such a floral tribute and waiting an appropriate length of time, the flowers are usually subtly handed to an attendant or lady-in-waiting. Quite a few garlands, posies and bouquets find their way into hospitals and care homes where they are gratefully added to other displays that are already in place. When Queen Elizabeth II came to the factory, just a few moments earlier than this photograph was taken, Mr C De Wit, the director of the Mullard Plant, was thrilled to see his daughter curtseying to Her Majesty as she presented her with a delightful display of orchids. These were not just any flowers, but special ones flown in from the fields in Holland the night before. The blooms came from a business that was owned by Mr De Wit's cousins, so this was a real family occasion. Workers formed a guard of honour as the Queen waved a gloved hand at the hundreds who downed tools for an hour in order to greet their special guest.

NOW THEN!
...the way we were

Each generation thinks of itself as 'modern', at every stage of life and yet we are all relics and momentoes of our own history. As time goes by, we try to hang on to our more modish and fashionable behaviour and attitudes, sometimes with the thought that we can defy the passing of time, despite our constant creation of 'the past' and our own archaeology. Most people, however, enjoy looking back and remembering with affection things done, things achieved and comparing the context of their early lives with

'improvements' made (sometimes!) in more recent times. Things often seem not to be as good as in the 'olden days', but most of the time we are not looking at a level playing field. Inevitably, many of our childhood memories, whatever our age now, are of endless summers and snow-filled

winters, a sort of 'local to us and historically appropriate version of Dylan Thomas's 'A Child's Christmas in Wales'! But for all of us, time marches on and as we get older, it seems strange that we find ourselves attempting to explain to an eleven year old god-daughter that there WAS life, of a sort, before computers, emphasising simultaneously our incredibly ancient origins! Wartime experiences and memories often define generations although with involvement in more recent conflicts, even this time line has had to be re-defined. The progress in radio and TV development has outstripped most people's imagination and provided a sometimes obsessive and questionable way of 'stuffing' our days. Until the middle of the twentieth century, children often had to use their own imagination, inventiveness and

All the equipment and artefacts used in play were simple, often loud and often extremely irritating in their use and application, but GREAT fun!

Left: In the 1950's, toys were still quite simple, for boys and girls. In a society that still placed the emphasis on women as home makers and 'children producers', toymakers were still making a lot of money from selling pretty little dolls to pretty little girls, banking on their softness for small, defenceless creatures in their own image. This wonderful picture, taken in 1950, shows two such little girls enjoying posing for a 'family' photograph, repeated no doubt, twenty years later, as the 'real thing'! Note the grittily determined, no-nonsense expression of the young lady at the back and the rather shyer, slightly myopic expression of the seated young lady with hair that, possibly, she has spent the rest of her life not being able to 'do a thing with'.!

Below: The influence of Errol Flynn in the 1940's is obvious here in a game involving bows and arrows. His playing of Robin Hood against Olivia de Havilland as Maid Marian, had a ground-breaking impact, for some little boys, that remained with them to their teenage years (and in some cases even longer!). Cinema has always had an influence on children's re-enactment and performance of stories and fables. Certainly children in the 1940's rarely complained about boredom or having 'nothing to do'. They simply grasped the nettle and worked out what they could turn it into and they did it together!

creativity. The streets were filled with groups of children of different ages pretending to be somebody, somewhere and something else. This was fun for most, freeing and gentle in its stimulation and engendered a relevant and satisfactory competitiveness conducive to learning.

Top left and left: Outside, including in the playground, improvisation was the name of the game. You didn't need a ball for football - a tightly bound bundle of rags or clothes would do. There were games that matched the seasons, conkers for example. Those determined to win used foul and dishonest ways to convert the simple conker into a hard and unyielding boulder to cheat their way to success! Later in the year it was marbles with wonderful 'glass beads' put to aggressive and destructive use to determine 'top dog'. There were also 'collecting' activities, usually involving cards with familiar faces, often footballers or film stars. Playground games were often determined by gender, with the differences usually marked by the polarising of physical prowess and single-mindedness on the one hand and a softer camaraderie and togetherness on the other.

Below: At one time, Monday was the traditional washday for many. For working class families, the burden fell upon 'mum'. Her role as a housewife meant that the day was spent boiling clothes in a tub and wringing them out through the mangle before pegging out on the line in the back yard. Before the days of sophisticated washing powders and rubber gloves, reddened hands were her reward and yet there were still beds to be made, carpets to beat and lino to wash. The children needed feeding and the evening meal had to be ready when 'dad' got home. It was hard work and there were few, if any, modern electrical appliances or 'white goods' to make the task of running the house any easier. Many families lived in terraced housing, some of it back to back, with outdoor 'lavvies', where you learned to whistle with one foot against the door in case someone else attempted to enter this little smelly enclave of privacy. Many houses still had a tin bath that was dragged in from the yard and filled with kettle after kettle of boiling water before family members took it in turn to soak themselves. This photograph, dating from the 1950's, shows a typical scene from life at the time; families and communities were close knit, sharing each other's joys and sorrows. It was quite common to lend a neighbour a helping hand in times of need and this was often more than just a cup of sugar. Friendships were often formed that lasted a lifetime.

Right: Conditions may have been grim on ocassions but there was usually time for a warm smile and friendly chat in the street communities around Blackburn. These were the days when people routinely left their doors unlocked - or open, without fear of someone running off with their television. Of course, they didn't have a television, but you know what we mean! These days the neighbourly culture which we used to take for granted has disappeared from many areas and some people seem to know the characters in the popular soap operas better than the people next door. It would be unusual, to say the least, to see a modern housewife scrubbing the pavement outside her house in the 1990s!

Below: This very 'typical' photograph, taken in 1960, reminds many of us how much we looked forward to that afternoon period which included 'games', particularly in the summer, the sound of willow on leather (not always!), the chance to compete and play in a team; the chap on the right doesn't look too pleased - maybe that's because he's carrying the rounders bat and is already worrying that he might have to play with the girls - NO WAY! - and it was ever so. From the well-developed greenery behind and the wearing of woolly tops one must surmise that we are looking at a late summer scene with the chance to impress and become part of the school team long gone. On the left of the picture the games teacher in her whites suggests it's summer and she will still demand 100% effort from everybody; after an initial scramble on the field to find a place on the boundary - less stressful, less running - provided you could throw, we all accepted our lot and relaxed the afternoon away, just glad, for once, to be out of the classroom.

Right: Fashion on the beach has surely changed a lot over the last one hundred years. Appropriate beach wear for men and women has moved with fashion. At one time, wool was, amazingly, seen as a suitable fabric for bathing outfits, despite its hideous stretching and shapeless qualities. Topless men on the beach were seen, at one time, as rather racy and promiscuous; yet, how would our Victorian forebears have dealt with the increased promiscuity of the last twenty years, with men AND women prepared to do and bare anything and everything on a beach; they would have been horrified never mind amused! In those days, young women were very bold if they revealed their ankles, knees and arms as they changed, on their parent's insistence, into their bathing attire inside a bathing

cart that could be wheeled into the water. Discretion was everything and a lack of it irreversible and so morality and prudence were established and preserved! A hundred years from now, however, we can be certain that OUR successors will look back with equal, if not increased, incredulity at our take on what is appropriate or not to wear on a beach!

Below: Out of necessity, road safety has become a major issue for all of us in our lifetimes and has been written into the school curriculum since the middle of the twentieth century. As we can

see in photographs from the turn of the twentieth century which appear in this book, children played games in the streets and rode their bicycles on the carriageway with little danger to life or limb. With the steadily increasing traffic in the 1930's, safety became an obvious and challenging issue and with accident statistics rising alarmingly the government of the day was obliged to take action. Driving tests were introduced, Belisha Beacon crossings appeared in towns and cities and that well-known bestseller, The Highway Code was formulated and published. After the Second World War, local councils turned their attention to the protection of children, who, at the time, lacked awareness of the dangers that existed in merely crossing the road or cycling to the shops. In this photograph taken in 1950, youngsters are given instruction on a model roadway system. Stop, look and listen were watchwords drummed into children together with instruction on how to signal correctly and how to use crossings safely. Too many young people lost their lives through ignorance and generally the population were happy to see schemes, such as cycle proficiency, being promoted. In later years, we saw the Tufty Club, the Green Cross Code and, frighteningly, a fully permed Kevin Keegan advising us on why it was NOT a good idea to run out from behind parked cars! Sometimes, it all seemed a little light-hearted, but at least it aided the retention of this information in the heads of children.

Below: When Ernest Evans asked whether it was a bird or a plane up there and answered himself by telling us that it was a twister, a craze was born that swept dance floors across the western world. He also made sure that countless numbers of children would be embarrassed at weddings, 21st dos and parties during the 1990s as their parents risked hernias and heart attacks attempting to twist the night away whilst their offspring raised their eyes to heaven. Evans was a fan of the 1950s rocker Fats Domino and used his name as the inspiration for becoming known as Chubby Checker. Oddly, his first big hit in Britain was in 1963 with 'Let's Twist Again', a follow up to 'The Twist', a record that only became very popular the following year. By 1963, when this couple attempted to keep their seams straight as they girated in the front room to the music from their Dansette record player, Chubby's star had already begun to wane. He switched to the limbo in an effort to promote another dance form, but with limited success. Reissues of his twist records have enjoyed new popularity in the intervening years, but have only added to the cringe factor for those forced to watch this couple 40 years on as they take the floor to the sound of 'Twist and Shout' or 'Peppermint Twist'. Sit down, mum, it's so gross.

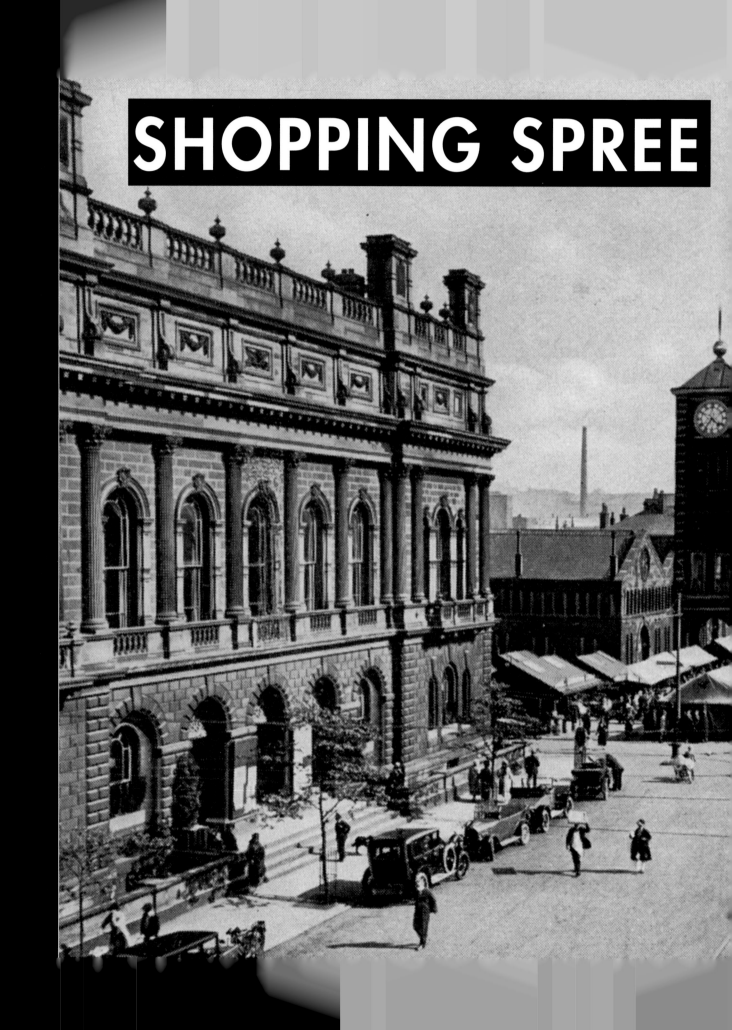

SHOPPING SPREE

The swinging 60s were famous for changes in musical tastes, a fashion revolution and bucking trends in morality and family values. Something else was swinging in the town centre at that time, namely the demolition ball. Out went the shops and buildings we knew so well as they were replaced by the featureless buildings of modernity. Blackburn was one of the first northwest towns to undergo, or should that be suffer, the wholesale slaughter of the past in its centre. It was not a quick process because building work, in one form or another, was not really completed until the 1980s. The shopping precinct and the tower block Town Hall extension are the main features of the so-called improvements. We must admit that they looked brighter and cleaner than the edifices they replaced, but what price can you put on character and individuality? These elements went forever. The old Town Hall was designed by James Paterson and built by Hacking and Stones. It opened in 1856 and can we really say that the new section will last for over 150 years as the old one has? The old market was also taken apart. This was not just a place to buy a variety of goods and fresh food, but an experience whereby friends could meet and chunter together as they enjoyed the background banter of the stallholders.

Perhaps the saddest part of the renovation and clearance project came when the magnificent clock tower was obliterated. It had stood on the King William Street side of the Market Hall for over a century, but it took just a few hours to have it reduced to mere rubble. The clock tower was something for which we had fond feelings and even the hardest of hearts was moved to regret when it disappeared in a pall of dust. The tower was almost unique in that it held a brass ball that was raised at 12 noon and was lowered again an hour later. When the ball arrived at the bottom of the mast, a gun was fired. The idea of a time ball came from a naval officer, Captain Wauchope. He had suggested erecting one on the bank of the Thames in London so that captains of sailing vessels could set their chronometers accurately. Wauchope took his suggestion to the Admiralty in 1833. It was approved and instruction was given to install a time ball on the top of a pole on the Eastern turret of the Royal Observatory at Greenwich and 1 pm decided upon as the time for the firing.

A number of towns and cities copied the Greenwich idea and arranged for a similar time ball to be sited in their locations. Our own Liverpool and America's Washington introduced them in 1845. Others appeared as far away as Australia and New Zealand over the next couple of years. Designed by T Flanagan, Blackburn's Market House, as it was originally known, opened in 1848. The tower or campanile

was 72 feet high and in 1877 a decision was taken to add its time ball, though it would hardly be an aid to shipping. Blackburn was about to become one of the few inland towns to boast such a device. Reid Brothers of London was commissioned to provide the ball and work began in March 1878, taking just two weeks to complete. The associated gun was built by W and J Yates, a firm of local engineers. The first use of the time ball and gun took place on 2 May, 1878. The one o'clock firing continued daily until 1903 when the mechanism failed. Nothing was done about it

until after the Great War, but in 1924 the time ball was set in motion once again. The gun continued to be in regular use until 1931 before being put into storage. It would be used to indicate the start of the two minutes' silence on Armistice Day in future years. The time ball made its last journey along its pole in December 1964.

The proposal to do away with the old market and hall was mooted at the start of the 1960s. This, combined with a new shopping centre, was seen as a way of modernising the town centre and revitalising the area by attracting new businesses to open retail outlets. It was also seen as providing a service to local residents. The River Blakewater had to be culverted as part of the redevelopment programme and many viewed the provision of a new market as a step forward. It has to be agreed that the old one was in dire need of modernisation, but traditionalists felt that the radical makeover was just too much too soon. They felt that some of the past could have been incorporated with the new, rather than just bulldozing the lot. The new market and hall were built by Leonard Fairclough Ltd and now cover 12 acres. The opening ceremony was held on 11 November, 1964, presided over by Alderman George Eddie. As this was also Armistice Day, some wag in the crowd suggested that the time ball's gun should be brought out of mothballs and turned on the redevelopment committee.

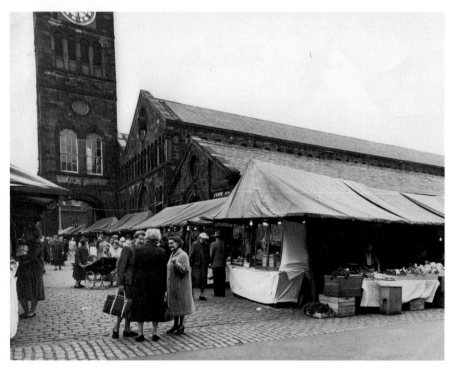

Above: Ladies and their fashion. Do you not love them? Every season has a new colour, a different length of hemline and a 'must have' outfit for a special occasion. This is the interior of the Co-op on Ainsworth Street. Here there is an ample selection of coats, dresses, tops and shoes. You could kit out an army with the goods on display. So why is it that the other half drags her long suffering hubby into here and back out again 30 minutes later? The answer is that she has not been to River Island yet. Then there is M&S to check out, and do not forget Dorothy Perkins. Guess what? Two hours later we are back in the Co-op purchasing the very jacket that she tried on all that time ago. By now, of course, tempers have become frayed and the whole experience has become another one to be ticked off on the list of things we should not do together. A lady's wardrobe is a wonderful place. It is seven times the size of the male counterpart. This is because she has to have a different set of clothes, handbags and shoes for every day of the week. Of course, if she was writing this piece then it would revolve around the scruffy nature of all men who are completely oblivious to any form of style and would live in the same jumper and trousers from one week to the next if allowed to do so.

Left: At the junction of Church Street and King William Street, a bobby on point duty was carefully shepherding traffic across this busy part of town. Behind him, the distinctive pillars above the awnings are typical of the stores erected for 'the tailor of taste', as Montague Burton became known. Men's clothing shops brought names to Britain's High Streets that became synonymous with affordable, but quality tailoring. Hepworth, John Collier and the Fifty Shilling Tailor had scores of outlets, but it is the Burton name that has lasted the longest. Meshe Minsky, a Lithuanian Jew who came to Chesterfield in 1900, founded the business. He adopted the surname of the town close to where he had established a small base. By 1910 he had opened four shops, but before long his business expanded to such a degree that he set up a huge factory in Leeds. In the 1920s and 1930s Burton was opening a new shop in a different town every month. The policeman in his white coat was a familiar figure at busy intersections before most of them were equipped with traffic lights. Note the Belisha crossing. The way across the street was marked out by studs. The now traditional black and white rectangles were not introduced until the early 1950s.

Left: King William Street has long been one of the main shopping areas in Blackburn. Much of the area was remodelled in the 60s and 70s and most of the retail outlets are now situated in pedestrianised parts. In the late 1940s, vehicles moved freely along this street, though shoppers did not have to contend with anything like the volume of traffic with which they had to cope as car ownership became more widespread. Although this was austerity Britain, the pavements were filled with locals. Perhaps many were just window shopping because rationing restricted the volume and variety of goods that could be purchased. Social commentators can look at the type of clothing that people wore when coming to town. Men wore jackets, shirts and ties. Most women wore some form of hat or headscarf above their coats and dresses. The couple heading south towards the bottom end of King William Street carried themselves well and their clothing suggests that they were middle class and did not get their hands dirty for a living. The lady looks very chic in her high belted coat. It was about this time that Christian Dior introduced his 'new look'. Out went dowdy wartime styles and feminine lines, longer hemlines and brighter colours were definitely in.

Above: This elevated view of the wholesale fruit market on Victoria Street was taken using the Town Hall as a vantage point. The main market covered an area of 12,000 square yards and boasted a total of 310 stalls. Some 180 of these were sited on the square on Victoria Street. When the fruit market was not in use the ground provided room for car parking. The very first markets in Blackburn would have been held in the grounds of the cathedral, but by 1101 formal permission was given to hold an organised market in the area enclosed by Church Street, Darwen Street, Mill Lane, Market Street Lane and Astley Gate. Robert de Lacy erected a Market Cross at the end of Church Street, but this was destroyed during the English Civil War in 1642. Sadly, no-one saw fit to replace it. De Lacy was also the prime mover behind the building of Clitheroe Castle. In 1803, as Blackburn started to increase in size because of the influence of the industrial revolution, control over the market was assumed by the Town Commissioners. They undertook the building of a new market hall in 1848, with an open market next to the Town Hall. A second hall and fish market were added in 1872.

Below and right: The tower block of the new Town Hall rises up above the shopping precinct, with British Home Stores being the main retail outlet that we can see. In the 1960s it seemed that every town in Britain had its centre remodelled. Blackburn was no exception. Old and, in many cases, treasured buildings were swept away in the drive towards modernisation. Concrete, steel and glass were the new kings of the building industry. It appeared that architects could only think in rectangles and straight lines. Little was done to make the new shops and offices have much in the way of individuality. Victorian planners who made sure that stone work had interesting reliefs, charming cupolas and carved designs must have been turning in their graves. Prefabrication took over from aestheticism as the byword. Sometimes, a visitor to a strange town could really feel at home when doing his shopping. After all, the town centre looked exactly like the one he was used to back home. The outlets had the same names and the layout of the mall was identical. No wonder that in 1984 Prince Charles was moved to describe the proposed extension to the National Gallery as a 'monstrous carbuncle'. Some thought that his criticism did not go far enough.

Left: It didn't begin to rival Blackpool Illuminations, but these Thwaites Arcade Christmas lights were a welcome and worthwhile attempt at getting shoppers into the Christmas spirit. The Thwaites Arcade was built in 1883 and had connections with the family of local brewers which shared the same name. The arcade formed an interesting link between Lord Street and Church Street. Tears were shed by some local people when it was listed for demolition in the redevelopment of the 1970s. It was finally pulled down in 1971.

Above: Thomas Fox and Sons is a long established fruit and vegetable wholesaler, currently based on Bruce Street, close to the railway to the east of Blackburn. In 1960, the stall at the market was well stocked with produce. The Redman's van belonged to another long-serving market trader family. This year was the start of the most prosperous decade of the century so far. Unemployment was falling and the job market was buoyant with opportunities for anyone willing to graft or show some enterprise. The war was now a distant memory and the Prime Minister, Harold Macmillan, was in a bullish mood. He had already told the nation that it was in a 'never had it so good' era and the economic figures supported him.

Right: Known as the helter skelter, pedestrian access from Ainsworth Street to some of the other shops and car parks is gained via this modern walkway. Even to those who complain about the faceless appearance of many of the concrete lumps called buildings, this circular design is appealing because it is different. More of this individuality and the traditionalists would have had less to grumble about. The 1970s' architects gave grumpy old men so much ammunition for their gripes. If only they had stopped to think in something other than box shapes. To use modern parlance, they should have thought outside the box instead. Shopping is now a cleaner and safer experience than it once was, thanks to pedestrianisation and more airy retail outlets. There is so much more choice as well. We have lost the personality of the old shops but have gained in the convenient way in which our shopping is now arranged. The pity of it is that the two were not married together.

Above: An unusual rooftop view of the interior of the indoor market which dates from 1963. The distinctive iron pillars will be familiar to many readers. All the stalls had a very similar frontage, strictly controlled by the markets management to ensure uniformity. The sights and sounds of the market area (not to mention the distinctive aromas found there) created indelible memories in the minds of the people who visited it. Market trading has been a feature of life in Blackburn for many centuries, and the quality an value of the goods on offer has attracted people into the town from many miles around

Right: Darwen's Market House and Municipal Buildings in a scene from the 1950s. The rooftops of the market area can be seen in foreground and several period motor vehicles are parked without restriction in the centre of the picture. Talking of restrictions, motorists were now able to buy petrol without coupons as petrol rationing had ended in May 1950. By 1958 yellow 'No Waiting' lines began to appear on the streets of our towns for the first time, much to the annoyance of motorists and some shopkeepers who predicted a decline in trade as a consequence.

BIRD'S EYE VIEW

Even though the war had ended, those living in towns that had been heavily attacked in bombing raids cast a wary eye up to the heavens whenever a plane flew overhead. Happily, the direct effect on Blackburn's housing, public buildings and industry had been limited as there was little here to be of interest to the Luftwaffe. The aeroplane from which this photograph was taken would have caused little consternation on the streets below. On 21 June 1949, the lens was pointed over the King William Street district in the foreground. The Town Hall and Central Library can be seen clearly. The site for the latter building on Richmond Terrace was purchased in 1871. In the following year, on 18 July, Mayor Thomas Bury laid the cornerstone. It opened in 1874 as a purpose built museum and library. There were also rooms set aside for the exhibition of art work. Ladies had their own reading room as it would not have been seemly for them to mingle with the men, nor did they want their husbands seeing which naughty novels they might have picked up. The building still functions as the town art gallery and museum, but a new library was opened on Town Hall Street on 1 September 1975 in the refurbished 1930 Co-op Emporium. The number of mill chimneys in the distance show that textiles were still important to the town, but the skyline would soon change as the economic climate altered.

A rooftop view of Darwen in the late 50's early 60's, looking towards the Market House and the Municipal Buildings. This panoramic scene shows the normally vibrant market area and the adjacent bus lanes from which tired shoppers and workers would catch the bus home from the Town Centre. Over Darwen was incorporated in 1878 and it is during this period between 1850 – 1900, that much of the town was built. Place-names, date stones in terraces, and the buildings made from local stone and brick reflect this. It was one of the first places in the world to have steam trams. Darwen, or Over Darwen, as it was called until 1879 was a Municipal Borough until 1974 when it joined into a new Authority with Blackburn.

The opening of the Manchester to Liverpool railway line in 1830 was the beginning of one of the most important revolutions in public and freight transport that the world has seen. Suddenly, stagecoaches and turnpike roads, along with barges and canals, saw redundancy staring them in their faces. The new wonder of the age spread rapidly as industrialists and entrepreneurs recognised the value of the railway to the nation's economy and to their personal profit. Both goods and people could be moved long distances at speed and in bulk. Journeys that had taken days were now completed in a matter of hours. The age of steam also helped change the environment in which people lived. Families, who for generations, had lived in one particular town or village, suddenly upped sticks and went to earn a living in a part of the country that was miles away from where they had been raised. Censuses in the latter years of the 19th century showed just how many had left their places of birth, compared with those contained in the figures compiled during the first national censuses. Blackburn, as a booming industrial centre, was keen to access the railway as soon as it could so that large quantities of raw materials could be brought into the mills and finished goods moved out as quickly as possible. The Blackburn and Preston Railway opened on 3 June, 1846.

Right: The aerial view of Larkhill shows the flats and housing development that make up this estate. St Alban's RC Primary School is in the centre of the photograph. Such new housing was the answer to the slum clearance programmes and redevelopment plans adopted by most councils in Britain during the 1960s and 1970s. The Second World War left us with much to do and little in the way of the wherewithal to do it. Outdated homes with poor facilities had more than had their day, but town planners wanted to change the face of society as well as replenish housing stocks. Large estates with their own pubs, schools, shops, clinics, play areas and community centres were built. Tower block apartments were included in order to save valuable space on the ground. There was mixed success for this type of venture. Some thrived as new, vibrant communities, but in other places they became social trouble spots. The 14-storey blocks built at Larkhill in 1964 provided 240 new homes, but some people living there lacked or missed the neighbourliness that had built up over the years in families who often worked and played together. Two of the towers, Pendle

House and Ribble House, were demolished in 2001. Bowland House was refurbished at a cost of £2.3 million and renamed Mount Pleasant.

Below: In the late 1930s, Garden Street Mill, on the left, was used as a factory manufacturing gas masks. This was emergency work that had to be completed quickly. Britain's readiness for war had been handicapped by the prime minister's foolish trust in Hitler's promises at the meeting in Munich in 1938. Chamberlain waving a little bit of paper that he thought meant 'peace in our time' is a pathetic sight even 70 years and more on. Even so, after the Germans stormed into Czechoslovakia it soon became obvious that we needed to prepare for the worst. There was a rush to get on a war footing both for hostilities abroad and defence at home. There was a real fear that an enemy would indulge in a tactic of using poison gas from bombs dropped by the Luftwaffe. Production of gas masks became a priority and, by the summer of 1939, every child had been issued with one. Adults also queued to buy them and classes were held by civil defence volunteers who instructed the general public in how to use them. The building was owned in Victorian times by John Carr and Smith Bowdler. The Garden Street Mill Company was formed in 1902 and continued its predecessor's work as a cotton manufacturer. In the photograph, we are looking down on Wensley Fold and the gasholders belonging to the gasworks. The Blackburn Gaslight and Coke Company was founded in 1818. The works on Addison Street, off Wensley Road, were built in 1870 and closed in 1946.

Left: The railway station in the foreground is an obvious point of reference. It is served by two lines. In 1847, the one to Bolton was opened, followed in 1872 by the line to Clitheroe. The station was covered by twin train sheds with a canopy that encompassed all the platforms. Sadly, this was allowed to decay and was replaced in 2000 during redevelopment work that resulted in extensive remodelling, though the old entrance was retained. Blackburn had been quick to respond to the idea of a railway line serving the town. Industrialists soon spotted the potential for moving goods and raw materials in bulk. Naturally, there was some opposition from those with a vested interest in the canals and turnpike roads. They knew that their financial stakes in these was at risk if the new mode of transport was a success. A meeting at the Old Bull Inn in late 1840 to discuss funding was inconclusive as objectors helped dampen enthusiasm, but evidence from other towns helped win the day for those who saw a rail network as a progressive step. An Act of Parliament in 1844 granted the right for the Blackburn to Preston line to be built and the age of steam locomotives arrived in this part of East Lancashire.

WORKING LIFE

Working underground was tough enough for adults, but notice how many of these workers were just young lads. Waiting at the pithead in the early 1900s, this gang was about to do a long and dangerous shift. Martholme Colliery, near Great Harwood, was one of scores of pits in the area. Working the coalface was filled with danger. If the cave-in did not kill you then the gas or an explosion might. Even if you survived these risks, lung disease or whitefinger awaited you in later life. The risks involved meant that miners worked as a closely knit community. Each individual's welfare was heavily reliant on his workmates. Carelessness or foolhardiness was not to be tolerated and woe betide anyone who brought matches or smoking materials below ground. In a few years' time, many of these men would take the king's shilling and sign up for armed service in the Great War, perhaps believing that this was an avenue of escape from the rigours of mining. Many were sadly and fatally disappointed. Martholme, sometimes known as Cock Pit, opened in 1848, but ceased production in 1930.

Above: Blackburn was a real cotton town. There used to be mills galore in and around the district, paying homage to the textile that brought great prosperity to the region. These ladies at Waterfall Mill, pictured enjoying the fun of being queen for a day at the time of the 1953 Coronation, did not share the wealth of the owners. However, they had jobs and in austerity Britain that was something for which they could be grateful. Unfortunately for them, the great days of the trade were behind them and the winding-up of companies was well under way. Waterfall Mill, at Queen Victoria Road, Mill Hill, was built in 1851 and was a handsome building. It was not at all like the dark, satanic mills of William Blake's poetry, but a well designed and attractive one with a semi circular pediment and arched windows. In its heyday it was run by John Fish Ltd, a cotton spinner who owned the mill during the period 1870-1939. At the start of the last century there were nearly 80,000 looms in operation in the local industry, but by the 1970s this had shrunk to a mere 2,000. The rot really set in as far back as the 1920s when India imposed a heavy duty on imported cotton goods. Despite a small boom just after the Second World War, it is ironic that cheap imports to this country from India, Pakistan and other Asian nations crippled what was left of our home grown textile trade. The mill is now home to a variety of industrial units.

Right: It was said at one time that school leavers need not worry too much about future employment as there was always a job at Mullard's for them. For very many years it was certainly a major and influential employer. It was also the sort of place where generations of workers earned their weekly crusts. People will recall friendships that were formed on the shop floor and where young love sometimes blossomed. Older readers who worked there and at similar plants will recall the sounds of 'Workers' Playtime' coming over the tannoys. It was a simple comedy and music programme that became part of the national fabric, serving the British population from the Blitz to the Beatles. First aired on the BBC Home programme on 31 May 1941, it was one of the first touring variety shows to be broadcast on radio. Initially granted a six week run, it went out from a factory canteen 'somewhere in Britain'.

Below and bottom: Being true Lancastrians, we like our ale. Two of the best known brewing names in the county had their bases in Blackburn. Father and son,

Thomas and William Dutton, founded their brewery at Salford in 1799, near to where the railway station would later be built. Unlike most ventures in the growing town, the Duttons' business was very slow in becoming established. By 1827 both the men were dead and the next in line was still a minor, so the company was run by trustees. It managed to survive, but the main thrust forward towards making the brewery a commercial success came when John Tattersall, the owner's brother in law, was taken into partnership in 1853. Dutton's began to expand, buying up smaller breweries, and the firm became an important part of the town economy for more than a century. As with so many others, though, it was eventually gobbled up by one of the giants. Whitbread took it over in 1978 and the brewery was demolished in 1986. Morrison's supermarket is now on the site. The Thwaites' story, however, still goes on. Seen here is the construction of its bottling depot, with the wholesale market in the background. This brewery clocked up 200 years of production in 2007 and remains fiercely independent.

Cobham Defence Communications
From Air to Airwaves

Cobham Defence Communications (CDC) based in Haslingden Road, Blackburn, is part of the Cobham Defence Systems Division, which is itself a wholly owned subsidiary of Cobham plc.

Cobham plc's origins go back to 1934 when Sir Alan Cobham founded Flight Refuelling Limited (FRL) to investigate Air-to-Air refuelling (AAR) techniques.

Alan Cobham, born in 1894, had a varied early career including a stint touring the country with the Berkshire Aviation Company, giving joy-rides in a war surplus Avro 504K. In 1921, he became the first pilot for the new de Havilland Aeroplane Hire Service.

Cobham established himself alongside other famous racing aviators after winning the 1924 King's Cup Air Race in a prototype DH.50. Chosen to accompany the Director of Civil Aviation, Sir Sefton Brancker, to India and Burma, they investigated the viability of setting up airship routes to the Far East. Their correct conclusion was that the aeroplane, not the airship would eventually win the day.

In 1926 Cobham flew from Rochester in Kent to London, via Australia, and finally landed on the River Thames in front of the Houses of Parliament before an audience of a million spectators. Alan Cobham was knighted immediately following his return to England.

An aviation innovator, Cobham operated a touring airshow – 'Cobham's Flying Circus'. In 1932 his skilled aerobatic pilots, wing-walkers, parachutists and novelty turns thrilled crowds across the country.

Sir Alan founded a new company; Flight Refuelling Limited (FRL) in 1934 to develop air-to-air refuelling equipment (AAR) and techniques that could be employed commercially.

Many landmark events followed - 1939 saw the first non-stop AAR crossing of the Atlantic; Imperial Airways 'C' Class flying boats refuelled by FRL's Harrow tankers.

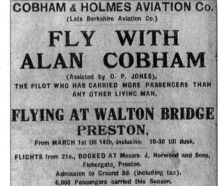

Top: Sir Alan Cobham. Left: Alan Cobham flies along the River Thames following his return from Australia, October 1, 1926. Above: Early advertising for Cobham & Holmes Aviation Co. Below: Royal Ordnance factory in the 1950s.

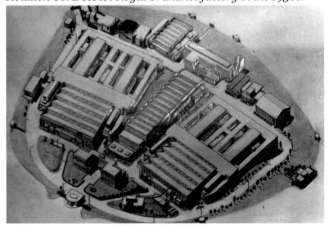

In 1948 FRL was the first British private contractor to join Operation 'Plainfare' during the Berlin Airlift to which the company provided twelve aircraft.

That same year the US Air Force used FRL 'looped hose' AAR equipment for its KB29 tanker fleet. In 1949 FRL invented the 'probe and drogue' method of AAR.

Over the following half century the Cobham group would become a world force in the field of aviation and defence, with involvement in every aspect of the industry, and with interests throughout the world - not least in Blackburn.

Lancashire's association with the aerospace and defence industries has its origins in the dark days leading up to, and during, the Second World War.

Steps were taken to guard against enemy attack on factories during the planned expansion of the defence industry by placing new facilities away from the vulnerable areas of South East England and the Midlands. The developments in Lancashire for example complied with this principle, as North West England was considered to be a relatively safe area.

Amongst the best remembered amongst this local wartime activity was the production of the Handley Page Halifax bomber by English Electric, a forerunner of BAE Systems.

On 10th April 1939 construction of the first hangar was started at Samlesbury, and completed in October of that year. This was the only hangar available for final assembly of early-production Hampden medium bombers. The construction of two tarmac runways had begun in August. As Hampden production was gathering momentum, English Electric received

instructions from the Air Ministry to prepare for the production of 100 Halifax heavy bombers. The Halifax was at this time in the very early stages of development at Handley Page and the prototype was not to fly for another eight months. The first contract for the Halifax was received in April 1940 and called for 200 aircraft.

The only part of that expansion programme not implemented by April 1939 was a flight test aerodrome. The site selected was at Samlesbury. The land had already been earmarked for a civil airport to serve the area, but had not been developed. It was situated on rising, open country, midway between Preston and Blackburn since labour could be recruited from both towns. By the end of the war some 2,500 Halifax bombers had been delivered.

Meanwhile, simultaneously with aircraft production in the area, were other related defence activities. Most importantly at Stopes

Brow in Blackburn a Royal Ordnance facility covering no less than 40 acres was built for the manufacture of mechanical anti-aircraft fuzes.

Royal Ordnance had played a crucial part in the defence of Britain for centuries. Since being established as the Royal Powder Mill in 1560 its explosive munitions and weapons would be used from the time of the Spanish Armada to Operation Desert Storm. The weapons

Top left: *Machining components during the war years.* *Above:* *Sailors fitting ROF Blackburn fuzes to 4.5' naval ammunition during the war.* *Below:* *Fuze test and inspection during the war. Note the tin hats which were for employees use.*

systems produced by Royal Ordnance would be used by the British armed forces and those of many nations worldwide.

Its Blackburn factory, known simply as the Fuze and later as ROF, appeared as war loomed in 1937. Blackburn was chosen not only because it was considered especially safe from air raids but also because government ministers had been impressed by the manual dexterity of the ladies at Roe Lee Textile Mill.

Building work was finished at the factory at Blackamoor in 1939, though defence work had begun before then in temporary premises. Only an artist's view of early factory conditions exists because cameras were not allowed. The factory was painted in daubs of brown and green to camouflage it from above and was protected by its own Home Guard unit. To further confuse the enemy, a decoy factory was erected on the moors. Inside the real factory two 12 hour shifts operated seven days a week. There was a proud day in 1941 when King George VI and Queen Elizabeth

made a visit. Workers were allowed to see them, but then it was straight back to work.

During the war the factory employed 5,000 people, including 3,500 women. They averaged some 15,000 fuzes every week working a 50 hour week.

Staff numbers were gradually reduced after the war until the workforce fell to around 2,000.

Top left: *King George VI and Queen Elizabeth visit the Royal Ordnance factory in 1941.* **Above:** *A view of part of the Auto Shop in the West Block in the 1950s.* **Below:** *The production of Mechanism Plates in Bay 2, 1957.*

After the important munitions work of the war, tasks like making the insides of alarm clocks seemed a come-down. For a while though, the factory was grateful to see any work. Soon, however, new defence work came in, together with high-tech design manufacturing with civilian applications.

Production capacity increased dramatically between 1951 and 1952 following major investment in equipment. 'Flow line' production was introduced and a plastic moulding capability established.

In the late 1950s an electronics capability together with mortar fuze, primer and tracer work was transferred to Blackburn from Maltby.

Electronic activities expanded further to include Launch Control posts for the Bloodhound missile subsystem.

The site's association with communications equipment began with the design and manufacture of the Miniature Control System for the RAF, and Larkspur equipment for army vehicles.

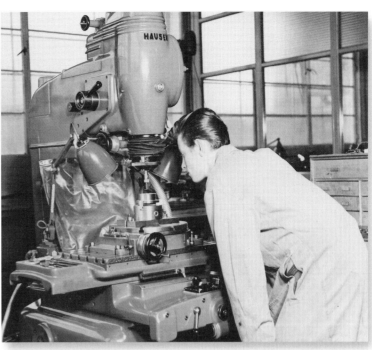

In the 1970s production began on a MoD order for the Clansman Harness communication system for army vehicles: this would be one of Blackburn's mainstays with production reaching a peak in 1979.

Royal Ordnance became a public limited company in 1985 and a wholly owned subsidiary of British Aerospace in 1987.

1985 and 1990 the workforce fell to just 1,200 as the traditional customer base shrank. The workforce was further reduced over the next four years to just 320, whilst the business introduced more competitive practices and looked for new markets, trying to decide how the technological skills of the remaining workers could be best used for new products.

Many people around Blackburn who noticed the demolition of the old Royal Ordnance Factory on Stopes Brow could be forgiven for believing that defence activities had ceased in the area.

But though 80% of the site disappeared for redevelopment, and past practices were abandoned, a vibrant business was functioning on Roman Road, thanks to the determination and skills of the staff of a new Royal Ordnance Electronics & Fuzes Business.

When spending on defence was reduced in the UK after the ending of the Cold War, Royal Ordnance was not idle. It took drastic measures, for example reducing its workforce. Between

Top: *Jig Grinding in the Tool Room in the late 1950s.* ***Above left:*** *A soldier with a Surface to Air missile, fitted with ROF safety and arming unit during the Falklands War.* ***Above:*** *Cross-sections of a traditional mechanical fuze assembly produced at the Blackburn Factory (A) and through the fuze, shell and cartridge-case (B).*

Overseas defence markets were very difficult to penetrate; however, a new portfolio was produced of products that would be amongst the best in the world in their niche markets. Some would become the standard by which competitive products were judged.

The traditional fuze business remained, much pared down and using electronic microcircuits instead of clockwork mechanisms. The components business too was sustained, introducing new products alongside the production of mechanical time fuzes for artillery and anti-aircraft ammunition. It would remain a multi-million pound complex with a wide range of military products.

A new simulation business would be developed, enabling troops to fight realistic battles in training and analyse the results without a real shot being fired. Perhaps the most important innovation would be the Royal Ordnance Vehicle Intercom System (ROVIS). Military vehicles are notoriously noisy, but communications between such vehicles are vital during military action. Royal Ordnance looked for a market to the USA, the

biggest user of sophisticated military equipment. Ordnance selected as a partner a large US company, Northrop Grumman, makers of the B2 Stealth Bomber. ROVIS would become the standard intercom for the military market.

BAE acquired Royal Ordnance from the MOD in 1989, before in turn selling the Electronics Division (which had relocated to a purpose built facility on Shadsworth Industrial Estate in May 2002) to Cobham in 2003.

Today Cobham plc is an international company engaged in the development, delivery and support of advanced aerospace and defence systems for land, sea and air platforms. The company has four divisions , which collectively specialise in the provision of components, sub-systems and services that keep people safe, improve communications and enhance the performance of aerospace and defence platforms.

Blackburn's Cobham Defence Communications (CDC) is part of the Cobham Defence Systems (CDS) Division. CDS designs and manufactures high power microwave components, sub-systems and integrated assemblies for national security, defence and law

enforcement markets, and provides advanced digital military vehicle tactical communication and information systems, soldier situation awareness and integrated navigation management tools to armed forces around the world.

CDC designs and produces modular fully digital tactical communications, control systems and situational awareness products to meet the most stringent operational requirements of users. The systems available from CDC are suitable for a wide range of platforms, ranging from light vehicles and boats through heavy armour to command posts and ships of varying sizes.

Top left: A Multi Axis Kitimura machining centre producing finished components. *Above:* Cobham's exhibition stand at the Farnborough International Airshow. *Above left:* An example of CDC's Vehicle Intercom System.

The Blackburn facility is the world's leading supplier of modular, rugged lightweight intercom products to its global customer base and has, to date, supplied over 120,000 systems, and continues to find new markets and customers for its systems every year.

Product innovation and the continuing design, development and re-engineering of its products, business and the supporting processes are continuously improved to ensure that the company meets its customers' requirement in terms of quality, cost and delivery.

CDC is also focused on meeting the customer's operational, and very importantly crew requirements, whilst maintaining a safe working environment for the crew and compatibility with the platform, its operating environment and the increased demands of the modern battlefield through customer partnership and strategic marketing networks.

CDC 's design centre and head office in Blackburn Lancashire is where, in addition to designing and producing the company product range, also offers a world-class Electronic Manufacturing service to the defence industry.

Production capability at the Blackburn facility is kept in line with the 'best in class' through competitive tendering and benchmarking activities with other defence producers. At Blackburn the company annually manufactures over 500,000 high-quality electronic circuits for export around the globe,

winning the Queen's Award for Enterprise in 2002 and 2007 and the East Lancashire Chamber of Commerce Export Awards in 2005.

In recent years employee numbers have doubled, through recruitment at the Blackburn facility and the acquisition of software, hardware and systems design business in Exeter, Devon, which currently employs in the region of 20 engineers and support staff. During this period sales quadrupled, due to demand for the company's products from the USA and other customers worldwide.

Growth was greatly helped by the success of the LV2 (Light Vehicle Variant Intercom) which saw demand rise from 1,000 to 8,000 units per month.

To achieve those performance levels the Management Team developed a strategy to improve all areas of the business by releasing the talents of all its employees.

The company also uses industry-leading Management Consultants and Cambridge University to develop best practice and to facilitate strategic reviews.

Today Blackburn and Cobham Defence Communications share a proud heritage having travelled together through the air to the airwaves.

Top left and right: At work at Cobham Defence Communications, Haslingden Road, pictured below and left.

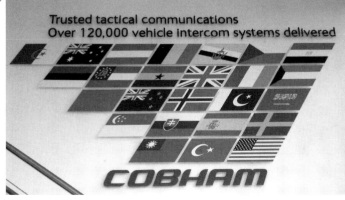

WH Bowker - Innovation, Performance, Reliability since 1919

The lorry became the icon of commercial haulage as the last century unfolded. The canals were long forgotten and, although rail travel was still heavily used, the improvement in road links meant that goods and materials could be moved ever more quickly and reliably via this means. With the building of motorways in the second half of the 20th century and the increasing volume that larger vehicles could handle, lorries became a vital part of the infrastructure of the nation's transport network and its economy.

The Bowker Group is among the leading heavyweights in this industry. The company has a large fleet of vehicles and trailers shared between operating centres in Preston, Hull and Zeebrugge. In addition to the warehousing and freight handling services that are provided, Bowker also owns BMW and Mini dealerships in Blackburn and Preston, along with one for Harley Davidson and Buell motorcycles.

All told, the company offers a full range of services from the use of a single delivery vehicle right up to packages for major distribution of goods and equipment. It has acquired a particular reputation in the field of transporting dangerous chemicals. Here it sets the standards for others to follow in a tightly regulated industry and has earned a formidable place in the ranks of distributors who are trusted for their reliability, efficiency and attention to detail.

Transporting loads safely and securely across this country and onto the Continent is a job for dedicated professionals and Bowker leads the way in its cutting edge delivery of such a service.

Modern lorries are smart and shiny, clean and powerful. They are a far cry from the chugging contraptions that

first rolled onto our roads immediately after World War I. Although a dreadful experience, war always accelerates technological improvement in certain areas. World War II laid the foundations for dramatic improvements in the aircraft industry.

The 1914-18 conflict, while introducing aeroplanes to a wider world, was particularly influential in opening people's eyes to the value of mechanised transport on the ground. It could be said that we went into the

Top left: *Founder, William Bowker. Above: During the war years William Bowker was taught to drive in a series of short lessons.* *Bottom left:* *The first year of trading, 1919.* *Left:* *A vehicle used for long hauls to London.* *Below:* *1926 and William Bowker embark with their first trunk to London.*

the serviceable ones were brought back from France for resale to the general public. Many ex-servicemen used the opportunity to invest their army gratuities into a fledgling road transport industry. William Bowker was just one such man who realised that he could not pass up this chance to be in on a commercial venture that seemed destined for greater things.

In 1919, he began in business from a base at 57 Craig Street in Blackburn by carrying fruit from the docks at Liverpool to his hometown market. He continued in a steady way for a number of years until another opportunity for advancement presented itself. It was born out of the misery of the General Strike of 1926 when millions downed tools and the railways ground to a halt.

trenches on horseback and came out of them in tanks, such was the speed of change. What is true is that the horse was still regarded as an important part of our transport culture in the early 20th century, but its day was done by the time the armistice was signed in late 1918.

There was an urgent need for road hauliers to move much needed goods long distances across Britain. William took the risk of committing himself and his finances to hiring other lorries, vans and drivers in order to move fruit and vegetables from Liverpool to London's Covent Garden. His courage paid

Born in 1893, William Bowker was the sixth of nine children. He left school at the age of 13 and went to work in the family fruit and vegetable business. Having spent eight years learning the trade, he answered Lord Kitchener's 'Your country needs you' call and was an early volunteer for the armed forces in 1914.

Top left: A section of Bowker's Leyland fleet leaving Liverpool with 3,000 cases of oranges for a 6 am delivery to Covent Garden, London. Above: Pictures from the 1930s and 1940s which was a period of building, progress and consolidation for Bowkers. Below: The Bowker fleet in 1954, a time for a new beginning for the company after the Second World War.

Like so many of his compatriots, William thought of it as a brief adventure. After all, everyone knew that it would be over by Christmas and this was a chance to both serve his nation and have the opportunity to visit Paris. He enlisted in the Royal Army Service Corps and was taught to drive in a short series of lessons that were conducted on London's Horse Guards Parade. Of course, his time in uniform turned out to be a terrifying four years, but he served with distinction driving ambulances and lorries that ferried vital ammunition supplies to the front. This was dangerous work, but he came through and returned home as one of those who vowed to help build a better land for himself and his family.

Thousands of lorries had been built by the government and

position at Holme Road, Bamber Bridge that took place in 1989 meant a greater co-ordination of the business. There had been much change along the way.

off and he was the first to establish overnight trunk movement in the whole of the United Kingdom. William was soon feted as the principal haulier for the Liverpool Fruit Importers Association.

WH Bowker Limited, as the company came to be known in 1941, developed as a family business. The founder was the governing director and two brothers and a brother in law worked with him. As trade increased and the company expanded, new premises were found at Stansfield Street. Bowkers stayed there until July 1949 before relocating to Hollin Bridge Street. By then, the company was working out of four sites, so the move from Blackburn to a seven acre, later ten acre,

1961
First steps into Europe

Despite the depression years of the 1930s, Bowker's more than just survived. It was able to progress trade by working for such local companies as Foster Yates and Thom, Henry Livesey, Northrop, Clayton Goodfellows and the Lancashire Cotton Corporation. Help was given to the war effort in the early 1940s as vital goods and equipment were moved across the country by a fleet of Bowker lorries.

Above pictures: WH Bowker have been offering an international service since 1961. Below: Following expansion in the 1960s the company opened a new depot in Hull in 1971.

combinations, authorised dealerships and the opening of the company's own rail terminal when relocation to Bamber Bridge took place. During the late 1970s and 1980s a third generation of Bowkers joined the firm as Bill junior, Neil and Paul came on board.

Although now a major force in the transport industry, the Bowker Group has never forgotten the family business ethic of service, integrity and loyalty. With 150 vehicles and 350 trailers, 500 employees and 400,000 square feet of warehousing it is a large enterprise with a big heart that has never forgotten its Blackburn roots.

The postwar Labour government introduced nationalisation on a massive scale. In 1949, it was the turn of the road haulage industry to come under central control. William Bowker had built up a fleet of 75 lorries and an excellent reputation to go with them in the 30 years he had been in business. The newly formed British Road Services (BRS) swallowed up his vehicles and WH Bowker Limited was left to trade just in warehousing. A partial change of heart came in 1953 when the now Tory government decided to sell off one third of BRS in small lots to licensed vehicle operators. William decided to rejoin the industry and recreate a legacy for his sons. Sadly, his return was short lived. William passed away in 1955 and his son, Bill, took over the reins at the tender age of 19. Bill's brother, Ken, would come into the fold as a 16 year old in 1960. By then, young Bill, thanks to a mixture of grit and determination, had overcome the drawbacks of crippling death duties and a small fleet of lorries that were in dire need of replacement. Somehow, the company survived, though few competitors would have bet on it.

Like their father before them, Bill and Ken had faith in their own abilities and a keen eye for an opportunity. They decided that Europe was ripe for development. In 1961, the first load for Singer Cobble was taken to Holland. The international operation was expanded during the 1960s, with the opening of North Sea Ferries in Hull offering even greater outlets. The first company depot in Hull was opened in 1971, with another following in Zeebrugge in 1976 as WH Bowker International was formed. Dedicated contract hire, providing 'in-house' fleets for manufacturers, was begun in 1978. The 1980s provided more business opportunities for expansion into lorry and trailer

Top left: WH Bowker's relocation to Preston in 1989. **Below:** *The company's UK distribution service.* **Bottom:** *Bowker's Mini, BMW, Harley-Davidson and Buell dealerships.*

Robinsons Holidays - From Charabancs to Comfort Class Coaches

Looking at the fifteen sleek and modern Comfort Class Coaches making up the current fleet of Robinsons Holidays of Great Harwood, it is hard to visualise where this all started in 1923. The Robinson family of Great Harwood were originally farmers who started up and operated their own coach company from their existing farm land and utilised their barn as their first garage. The same land today (Park Garage at Great Harwood) is still used by the company, but has grown from one small garage building to three, including a workshop for the company's own maintenance staff and an indoor 'wash' area for the coaches. There is also an office and administration area on this site.

Today's passengers, travelling in these luxury coaches can either be picked up from one of over 130 departure points or take the option of door-to-door transport from their own homes and they don't need to handle their luggage as there is an 'integrated luggage handling service'. The passengers of 1923 would have had a far less luxurious ride to their counterparts today, no 'comfort class' for them, or reclining seats, air conditioning or toilet facilities! Instead they would be seated in the back of open lorries with solid tyres and fixed bench wooden seats for their day trips to the seaside. There is documentary evidence of a day trip for 300 passengers from the Bolton Co-op who travelled with Robinsons in such charabancs over the Pennines to Scarborough for the day in the mid 1920's. Those suffering from travel sickness in these early forms of coach

The ANNUAL HOLIDAYS.
W. Robinson & Sons' Glorious Motor
Char-a-banc Tour
TO
ABERYSTWYTH
and WEST WALES.

FIRST-CLASS BOARD, INCLUDING 3 MEALS PER DAY—

Seven Days for £6/17/6 No Extras.

Top left: Frank Kemp stands proudly in front of his 1950's Bedford SB coach. *Above:* Advertisement for a pre-war Charabanc tour to Aberystwyth - with the promise of 'all weather equipment and rugs' but 'only a small amount of luggage allowed'! *Below:* A Robinsons coach of the 1950's - it has a Moseley engine with a Plaxton body.

travel were encouraged to wrap their upper bodies in brown paper to ease the queasiness!

There is also evidence of a charabanc tour offered pre-war to Aberystwyth, 7 days for £6-17s-6d or £6.87p in today's money. The tour was advertised on a poster as running with a 14-seater pneumatic-tyred coach which would clearly

have been slightly more comfortable than the previous solid-tyred versions mentioned above. By this time the charas were advertised as being fitted with 'all weather equipment and rugs'! 'Only a small amount of luggage allowed'.

In 1948, Robinsons was bought by the family-owned Holdsworth Group and is still under the same control. The name W.Robinson and Sons (Great Harwood) Ltd was retained. The coach livery in that era and until quite recently, was green and black and the initials 'WRS' were plainly visible on the sides of the coaches. The slogan 'Carefree Holidays' became synonymous with the Robinsons' touring experience. More recently this has become 'Every Mile's a Smile' – which can be seen emblazoned on the sides of the

current fleet, the livery of which is now blue with the Robinsons' name in graduated yellow and orange.

Post-war in 1951 a similar break in Torquay to that offered to Aberystwyth pre-war and mentioned above, would have cost £14-14s-0d. According to the 1951 brochure, this 7 day holiday would include 800 miles of touring, and include excursions to Dartmoor and Buckfast Abbey. You would have been staying at one of the company's own hotels - the Dorchester Hotel in

Top: Group photographs like this were typical of tours of the 1950's and 60's- this one shows the party, the driver (Frank Kemp - front row far right - seated), and the coach - a 1950's Bedford SB. **Left:** *An inside view of a typical 1950's Robinsons coach - taken from the 1951 brochure - absolute luxury for its time.* **Below:** *A picture of how the original Bedford SB of the 1950's with a butterfly front, would have looked in its green and black Robinsons livery.*

provided. All touring coaches provide reclining seats, with reduced seating to give extra leg room, together with air conditioning and toilet/washroom facilities.

In 1982 Robinsons purchased another local coach company, Ribblesdale Coachways. One of their main contracts was providing transport for the pupils of Westholme School, which Robinsons continue to do.

Robinsons passengers throughout the years have tended to stay faithful to the company, possibly because of its family origins, ethos and name which have remained. Most passengers travel by feeder coach to the

Torquay, whose main unique selling point of the time was that it boasted 'an Electric Lift'. Ten years later, according to the brochure for that year, the same holiday would have only risen by £2, but by then the same hotel was not only boasting 'Electric Lift' but now also a 'cocktail bar, ballroom and television'. This was one television for the whole hotel, not each room as it would be today! By 1971, an additional feature offered was 'entertainment in the hotel most nights', plus it was licensed. Even at the height of the season, this was a bargain 7 day holiday for £27 and 15 shillings. A further 10 years had seen inflation and decimalisation hit the nation and the 7 day holiday was, in 1981, £110 at the height of the season. With increasing inflation over the years, a high season seven day holiday to Torquay costs from £339 in 2009. This is still a very competitive price.

Robinsons has prospered because it is able to keep up with the times. It built up a client base of loyal customers, thanks in no small part to the reliability of its service and the increasing variety of what could be

*Top: Two typical Robinsons coaches of the 1980's - both Leyland Tigers in the then familiar green and black livery-picking up passengers. **Above right:** 1985 Holiday Fair - members of Robinsons Holidays promotions team showing interested passengers the British and European Tour Brochures - The board features a 14 day tour to Yugoslavia and incorporates several other countries. **Right:** Retired but not too old for restoring to its former glory! - the 1956 Bedford SB XTB 91 on its way home again to Robinsons. It was tracked down by Robinsons employee William Brayford, an enthusiast and collector.*

from coach driving, George acted as a part-time supervisor, welcoming passengers and assisting at the Lymm interchange. Similarly, the late Ron Devereux worked with George at Lymm in his later years. He was Office Manager at Robinsons for many years before that, his son, Barry, is now the General Manager of one of Robinsons own hotels – the Abbey Lawn in Torquay.

One of the existing staff, William Brayford has been at Robinsons since 1984, as a young boy helping out and then as a fitter and a driver. William followed in his family's footsteps. His father, Bill, joined Robinsons as a driver in 1972 and is still there driving today. William is a keen collector of all memorabilia and photographs connected with Robinsons. Amongst many other Robinsons' artefacts, William has tracked down two coaches which were previously owned by Robinsons. The more 'modern' coach of the two is a 1983 Leyland Tiger and is still in perfect working order. The other is a 1956 Bedford SB, which hopefully will be restored to its former glory.

interchange point at Lymm in Cheshire or other central points, from as far north as Barrow and as far south as Birmingham. An increasing number of passengers are making use of the door-to-door service, which picks up at home and goes directly to the main tour coach. Passengers frequently return year after year and many have several holidays each year, finding comfortable surroundings and companionship. Robinsons continue to update the coach fleet, and build on the popular holiday destinations, seasonal and festive breaks and private hire availability to suit the needs of existing and new passengers. Robinsons 'tours' nowadays are much more likely to be luxury coach holidays offering tours not only throughout the UK but also throughout Europe – the 2009 brochure, for example, offers trips as far afield as Germany, Austria, Italy and Slovenia.

Many of the drivers and other staff have also remained loyal to Robinsons and have been able to provide photos and memories of tours of former decades to contribute to this article. Frank Kemp was one such driver who was with Robinsons from the 1950's. When Frank retired from driving he remained with the company doing sales promotions and holiday fairs and until recently, worked in the company's office at Great Harwood. Similarly, George Carter also spent most of his working life driving for Robinsons. After retiring

*Top: A MAN powered Neoplan Starliner coach. **Below:** The latest additions to the Robinsons fleet are two Plaxton bodied Volvo B12M coaches with Paul Godwin, Engineering Manager.*

Blackburn College - Years of Learning

Education is important in every society, but few communities have valued education as highly as the residents of Blackburn. And in the closing decades of Queen Victoria's long reign the demand for educational opportunities reached a new high.

For more than 120 years Blackburn College, now East Lancashire's largest post-sixteen education provider, has been meeting the educational and training needs of the area's industry and commerce, as well as other sectors of the community. In 2007 the College was declared 'outstanding' by Ofsted. In 2008 it was awarded a Beacon Award for its excellence in teaching and learning. The College is consequently among the top five per cent of all Learning and Skills Council funded providers. Today the College offers a wide range of courses - from A Levels to vocational courses in Hair and Beauty, Childhood Studies, Public Services, Construction, Music, Media and Textiles through to Foundation Degrees, Degrees and Professional Qualifications.

The idea of founding Blackburn College is attributed to two local men. One of them, W.E. Bickerdike, was a manufacturing chemist in Oswaldtwistle; he had a particular interest in technical education after seeing it at work in Germany in the early 1870s.

Whilst in Berlin in 1872 Bickerdike was impressed by the importance that was attached to scientific instruction there, something which was in marked contrast to the relative indifference displayed towards it in England.

Bickerdike's early attempts to enthuse local people with the idea of opening a college in Blackburn initially fell on deaf ears. Many local businessmen were opposed to the provision of education for the working classes and felt that enough was already supplied by the Mechanics' Institute and various

Above: *The empty site on Blakey Moor in 1887.* ***Below:*** *The Technical College, completed in 1894.*

private colleges. In 1886 there had been a public meeting to discuss the foundation of a technical school, but there was so little support that the meeting had to be abandoned.

W.E. Bickerdike's luck changed however, when he joined forces with the Mayor at that time - Edgar Appleby – and linked the venture with the forthcoming Golden Jubilee of Queen Victoria in 1887.

The idea for a college caught on, and prominent local people soon became involved in the organisation and, more importantly, the financing of the project. A subscription list was opened, and about £15,000 was given voluntarily to build the school. Edgar Appleby, the Mayor, made substantial personal donations to the fund and stood for office a second time in order to see the project through. There remained however, an undercurrent of opposition. As W.E. Bickerdike later said "some of the old and very conservative people thought it was throwing money away".

A suitable site was chosen on Blakey Moor and building work commenced on this major undertaking. May 9, 1888 marked two milestones in the history of Blackburn. Firstly it was the day of the first ever Royal Visit to the town. Thousands of local people gathered to catch a glimpse of the Prince and Princess of Wales and memories of the occasion would be recounted for many years to come.

The future King and Queen were transported along Preston New Road in the State Carriage flanked by mounted lancers in their immaculate uniforms.

The second milestone was, of course, the laying of the foundation stone for Blackburn's first public college, and the start of an era of opportunity for ordinary people based upon merit and achievement. The actual laying of the stone was done inside a huge marquee.

Inside the foundation stone was placed a bottle containing coins, local newspapers and an inscription on vellum. Afterwards the Prince of Wales was made the first honorary freeman of the Borough of Blackburn. There followed a grand lunch in the Town Hall at which the Prince spoke about his support for the concept of technical education and its importance to the success of manufacturing industry. The Prince and Princess of Wales left the area during the afternoon, and local people continued to celebrate into the night with a fireworks display in Corporation Park. In 1891, three years

after the laying of the foundation stone, the first students moved into the building. Work was almost complete by that time. A wide range of subjects was taught, including Chemistry, Art, Building and Physics; particular emphasis however, was placed on Textiles and Engineering.

Many of the classes were held in the evenings after most of the students had completed their day's work in the local mills and factories. The courses were accessible to everyone, but not free. A fee of ten shillings (50p), a substantial sum in those days, was required in advance from students as a minimum payment for participation at this new seat of learning.

Soon afterwards financial assistance came from Blackburn Council, which was to be involved in the running of the College from that time on.

This page: 1940s views in the Weaving Shed (top left) woodwork class (left) and typewriting class (above).

The first couple of decades were difficult in terms of the organisation and running of the College. The result, in 1903, was that the College was taken over by Blackburn Education Committee and renamed Blackburn Municipal Technical School. By 1909 there were only 50 day-time students, but a massive 1,300 evening students attended the school. The evening classes were largely attended by apprentices from local companies.

Progress continued over the years and by 1950 there were 4,000 students on the roll of what was by now the Blackburn Municipal Technical College and School of Art. Soon it became clear that more room was needed to accommodate the growing number of students.

New buildings were commissioned and the foundation stone was laid by Lord Derby in 1954, in a large area between Nab Lane and Montague Street. The Feilden Street buildings were constructed in three phases between 1953 and 1963, and officially opened in 1964 by Lord Robens.

The textile industry dominated the town for many years, but as it contracted, the study of textile manufacturing disappeared from the College syllabus. In the mid-1960s, the name was changed to Blackburn College of Technology and Design, but when the College became the main provider of tertiary education in the borough in 1984, it was shortened to the more familiar Blackburn College.

As the College continued to grow, more new buildings have been added to the campus: the Nab Lane building in 1971, the School of Art in 1984, the renovated Blakey Moor school and, in 1988, the Technology Centre.

In 1988 when the College celebrated its centenary, the highlight of the year was the visit from His Royal Highness the Prince of Wales in June. He came to the College and removed the bottle from the foundation stone which his great great grandfather had placed there a hundred years before. The contents were intact despite rumours that the coins had been stolen by workmen during the construction of the Victoria Building. A 'time capsule' to represent 1988 was prepared by local school children and placed inside the stone by Prince Charles. In 2003 work began on an extension to the

Top left: Prince Charles' visit to Blackburn College during Centenary Year, 1988. Above: The new Technology Centre in 1988 which at the time had the most up-to-date computing facilities. Below left: A view of St Paul's Gardens and the site of what will now be the new University Centre in 1956 from the roof of the Feilden Street Building. Below: An artists impression of the University Centre set for completion in September 2009.

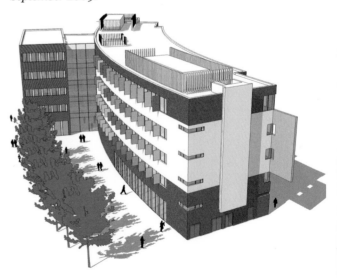

original Victoria Building on Blakey Moor. Work on the New Victoria Building was completed in 2005 and officially opened by the Queen's cousin, the Duke of Gloucester.

The new extension cost £4.4 million and created specialist teaching facilities for the College's Hair and Beauty, Hospitality and Business departments, including a 120-seater student-run restaurant – 'Scholars' - and state-of-the-art hair and beauty salons.

Meanwhile it had become apparent that a large part of the College was no longer fit for purpose, and in September 2007 the first phase of the College's multi-million pound Master Plan to create a new world class campus was opened.

The new £8.8 million St Paul's Centre houses the two areas of Sixth Form and Computing. Phase two – a new £13 million University Centre – is expected to open in September 2009 and further phases will include a new

Motor Vehicle building, a brand new core building followed by the demolition of the existing Feilden Street building.

A final phase of redevelopment will see the original Victoria Building sympathetically refurbished and upgraded with a new roof, windows and structural work as well as updating the Creative Arts building.

From modest beginnings the College now serves over 20,000 students of all ages, backgrounds, abilities and interests.

Today in the 21st century Blackburn College campus has physically changed beyond recognition since it was founded in the reign of Queen Victoria, yet, crucially, the overriding aim of being the prime provider of the community's educational and cultural needs, in support of local employment and commerce, remains unaltered.

Top: *Blackburn College's reception area.* ***Left:*** *This diagram shows the phases of the Master Plan to create a new world class campus.* ***Below:*** *A time capsule placed by Blackburn College on 7 September, 2007 at the opening of the new St Paul's Centre.*

Queen Elizabeth's Grammar School
Learning to be of Service

The school was founded as a free grammar school at Blackburn by Thomas Stanley, the 2nd Earl of Derby, and received its Royal Charter from Queen Elizabeth I in 1567. It was not until 1884 that it moved to its present site, half a mile to the west of Blackburn town centre.

The site, bounded by West Park Road, Dukes Brow, and the cricket field of the East Lancashire Club, has been likened to a small university campus. The school's excellent Harrison Playing Fields are a mile away, at Lammack Road.

'**D**isce Prodesse' is the Latin motto of Queen Elizabeth's Grammar School in Blackburn. The words translate as 'learn to be of service'. The school and its pupils have been learning to be of service throughout five centuries, ever since the school was founded in 1509.

Queen Elizabeth's, which today educates boys and girls from the age of three to eighteen, is a selective 'HMC' school, proud of its ability to prepare pupils not just for university but also for life.

In addition to providing high quality teaching and support to enable pupils to achieve academically, QEGS (as the school is popularly known) offers a wide range of extra-curricular activities that help to produce rounded and confident young men and women.

All this is a long way from QEGS' relatively modest beginnings as the chantry school to the Parish Church of St Mary the Virgin (now Blackburn Cathedral) in the centre of the town. There it remained until the need to build a new church required the school to move, first to a temporary home in nearby Market Street Lane and then in 1825 to the 'fresh air of the country' in Bull Meadow, just outside the town. The school building and the adjoining Headmaster's House can still be seen on what is now Freckleton Street, though having now become commercial premises.

At the time of the relocation to West Park Road, and for some 20 years thereafter, Blackburn Grammar School had fewer than 100 boys on its roll, though many went on to make their mark both nationally and internationally – John Garstang in archaeology, Sir Harold Derbyshire and Sir Benjamin Ormerod in law, Sir Ernest Marsden in physics and Pomfret Kilner in plastic surgery. Yet more went on to 'be of service' in the two world wars and the names of those who died are recorded on impressive memorials in the school's dining hall.

Top left: Pupils donning mortar boards pose for the camera at Freckleton Street, circa 1874. *Left:* Milk distribution outside the old gym, 1950s. *Above:* The Charter Window at QEGS.

Among many distinguished former pupils to have passed through the doors of Queen Elizabeth's in recent decades are designer Wayne Hemingway, TV presenter Krishnan Guru-Murthy, music promoter Yvette Livesey and professional golfer Nick Dougherty.

Traditionally strong in teaching science subjects, the school can also point to excellence in many other curriculum areas, including Art, Modern Languages, Classics and Mathematics. Drama is always of a high standard, and in sport. QEGS is becoming renowned for its netball teams as well as its long-standing prowess at football and cricket.

The school expanded in numbers during the 20th century, and formally became known as 'Queen Elizabeth's Grammar School, Blackburn' in April 1933, during the Headmastership of Arthur Holden. The science buildings, opened in 1958, are named after Mr Holden, who led the school for nearly 30 years.

Further development of the school site has taken place periodically over the last half century, to meet the new demands of teaching and of increased pupil numbers. Her Majesty Queen Elizabeth II performed the formal opening of the new Queen's Wing in November 1987 and the school's on-site swimming pool and new Sixth Form Centre were opened in the following decade.

The boys and girls being educated at Queen Elizabeth's today keenly follow in the school's tradition and still strive to 'be of service'. The fundraising and practical help they give to charities and those in need illustrate clearly the determination to make a difference which has always been the hallmark of a QEGS student.

Top left: Presentation of a silver vase to Her Majesty the Queen at the opening of the Queen's Wing in 1987.
Left: A reunion lunch in Big School, March 2007.
Right: The Early Years Department which offers the best possible start to boys and girls aged 3-6. **Below:** *A bird's eye view of Queen Elizabeth's Grammar School.*

In 2001, QEGS became fully co-educational (having welcomed girls into its Sixth Form since 1976) and the following year opened an Early Years section, which educates boys and girls between the ages of three and six.

Now, under Simon Corns, who became Headmaster in 2007, the school has over 700 pupils and maintains its enviable record of enabling students to obtain places at the leading universities.

Gillibrands

From Horses to Four Wheel Drives - 150 years of Vehicle Repairs

The company survived the inter-war depression and emerged well-equipped to exploit the huge demand for building and repairing motorised vehicle bodies.

Thomas Gillibrand was the mainstay of the business until his death in 1924. As well as being a highly respected businessman in the town, Thomas was closely connected to Blackburn Rovers, becoming a Director and Vice President of the Club.

In 1950, the business was bought from the Gillibrand family by Thomas Ellis, who had worked for the firm as an apprentice in the 1920s before gaining lots of experience by working at a number of other local coachbuilders.

On 4th July 1952 the company was Incorporated and officially became T. Gillibrand (Blackburn) Ltd.

In 2009, Gillibrand Accident Repair Centre, based in St Clement Street, Blackburn, celebrated an astonishing 150 years in business. The firm was established in 1859 by Mr J.Gillibrand in a small workshop on Longton Street in Blackburn, close to where the business is still located. He ran a wheelwright's shop and a blacksmith's forge and built horse-drawn carts. From the outset he provided a vehicle repair service.

The founder's sons, Thomas and Henry, ran the business towards the end of the 19th Century and described themselves as 'Wheelwrights, Blacksmiths and Shoeing Smiths'. In 1891, Thomas Gillibrand moved the business from Longton Street into a workshop on Cherry Street. Thomas wanted to build a family home there, but never did so. Over a hundred years on, the business still uses the same site.

In the early 20th century, whilst still building and repairing horse drawn carts, the firm began to specialise in pneumatic equipment for horse-drawn and tractor-drawn vehicles. As the company developed, it became ideally placed to take advantage of one of the biggest commercial opportunities to present itself at the time - the advent of motor transport.

Top left: *Early T. Gillibrand letterheads.* **Bottom:** *A horse-drawn cart made by T. Gillibrand.* **Above:** *Three Borough of Blackburn Cleansing Department Vehicles in the late 1960's .*

It was around this time that Gillibrands started repairing motor cars as well as building, repairing and painting commercial vehicles. The two businesses ran successfully alongside each other for the next fifty years, though the main business was still that of vehicle body building, which often involved creating vehicle bodies to the customers' own specifications.

As well as running a busy coachbuilding and car repair firm, Thomas Ellis was a dedicated Labour Councillor. He was the Chairman of a number of Council Committees and also the Leader of the Council for a number of years. His long service for the local ward of St Jude's, was marked by his appointment as Mayor of Blackburn in 1972.

In the early 1960's, Thomas Ellis was joined by his elder daughter Margaret and his son-in-law David Weddle. The company became known as Gillibrand Motor Bodies and

David and Margaret Weddle worked there together for over forty years, with David becoming the Managing Director.

Gradually, as cars became more and more popular and most families seemed to have at least one, car repair became the more prominent business.

Because of their large premises and years of experience in this field, Gillibrands were again ideally placed to take advantage of the next big shake-up in the vehicle repair Industry. During the early 1990's, Motor Insurance Companies started to appoint "Approved Repairers" and developed national networks of repairers who could provide their policyholders with a range of standard services.

At the turn of the century, the business stopped building vehicle bodies and is now entirely dedicated to the demands of the Accident Repair Industry.

Though Gillibrand's still bears the name of the original owners it is now owned by the Weddle family and managed by brothers Michael and Peter Weddle, grandsons of Thomas Ellis.

To maintain its position as one of the region's leading Accident Repair Centres, the company has invested heavily in training, new equipment and the building itself. In 2001 the office and reception areas were completely refurbished and most recently a quarter of a million pound investment was made in the Paintshop.

In 2008 Gillibrand's was awarded the BSI Kitemark 'PAS125' - the highest standard of quality within the Accident Repair Industry.

Now known as Gillibrand Accident Repair Centre, the company is an Approved Repairer for Insurance Companies such as Norwich Union and Royal & Sun Alliance, and is also Approved by a number of leading Vehicle Manufacturers.

Gillibrand Accident Repair Centre has survived major changes to modes of transport, repair technology and customer expectations. Who would have thought that a firm which began by putting shoes on horses would end up with 40 courtesy cars!

Above left: *Thomas Ellis, who purchased the business in 1950.* **Left:** *Former Managing Director, David Weddle, pictured in the 1970s.* **Above:** *A view inside the works in the 1970s showing a number of ambulances and commercial vehicles.* **Below:** *A bird's eye view of Gillibrand Accident Repair Centre in 2007.*

Heritage - Enveloping the World

Envelopes are something we all take for granted. Yet millions of them are used every day. Until the advent of the Penny Post however, few envelopes were used. Previously letters were simply folded over and sealed with wax, the address being written on the outside of the letter.

Envelopes were at first manufactured individually by hand, a laborious and time-consuming operation.

The first patent for an efficient, automatic, envelope-making machine was registered in England in 1845. It was granted to Edwin Hill, the brother of Sir Rowland Hill, well known for his reform of Britain's postal service and the introduction of the Penny Post in 1840.

In 1851 Edwin Hill and Warren De La Rue exhibited an improved version of Hill's earlier machine at the Great Exhibition held at the Crystal Palace in London.

In the century and half since the Great Exhibition massive strides in envelope-making technology have been made. And few firms in the world have made better use of that technology than Blackburn's Heritage Envelopes Ltd based in Davyfield Road, a company which produces around three billion envelopes every year using some of the most advanced machines in the world.

Heritage Envelopes Ltd was founded in 1985 by John Jackson and David Sears. Their small enterprise was based in Horwich, Greater Manchester.

In the first year turnover, using a single Smithe Rema envelope-making machine, was just over half a million pounds.

The business became a limited company in the following year, with David Sears' father Tom Sears as its Managing Director.

In the second year turnover reached £1 million, and the firm moved to the team's home town of Darwen. In 1987 a second Smithe Rema machine was acquired and turnover rose to £1.2 million.

The following year yet a third machine was bought.

In 1989 David Sears' brother Mark joined the firm as an adjuster and a fourth machine was installed in the growing factory.

Tom Sears passed away in 1990.

Annual turnover had now reached £2.5 million.

In 1994 Mark Sears became a Director and in 1996 a shareholder.

Yet another family member, Martyn Salt, David's brother-in-law, joined the firm as a warehouseman. The next year a fifth machine helped push turnover to £3 million.

By 1995 David's son-in-law Trevor Whittaker had joined the company as a packer. Larger premises were now needed, and in 1996 the growing business moved to Lower Darwen where a

*Top: Founders, John Jackson (left) and David Sears. **Above left:** The company's first machine a Smithe Rema M/c. **Below left:** Tom Sears, Managing Director from 1986 to 1990. **Above:** Mark Sears, Joint Managing Director who joined the company in 1989. **Below:** Heritage Envelopes' first WD 102, acquired in 1999.*

powerful second-hand Winkler and Dunnebier 102 machine was installed.

The following year three more used WD 102s were bought, and turnover reached £6 million. Yet another three pre-owned WD 102 machines were bought in 1998 and the original Smithe Rema machines taken out of production.

Ian Walmsley joined the company as Sales Manager in 1999, John Jackson became Operations Director and Mark Sears moved on to Sales & Technical Director.

With business booming a move was made to new 100,000 sq ft purpose built premises in Blackburn where turnover was soon pushed to over £8 million.

That year the first brand new WD 102 machine was installed. Two more were acquired in 2000, as were two 'Diamond' over-printing machines.

In 2001 turnover reached £14.5 million. The company exchanged its Diamond over-printers for machines from Winkler and Dunnebier - and two old WD 102s were replaced by new ones, as were two more WD 102s in 2002.

A four colour over-printer was acquired in 2002. By now Trevor Whittaker was Production Director, Ian Walmsley Sales

Director, Stuart Bromley Finance Director and Martyn Salt Logistics Director.

In 2004 with turnover of £19 million, Heritage made its biggest commercial decision going into partnership with GPV Groupe.

In 2007 with the takeover of full control by GPV, a new management structure was put in place. David Sears would become UK Vice President, Mark Sears and Trevor Whittaker Joint M.D's of HERITAGE & Sister Co CHAPMAN ENVELOPES. Richard Lucas was appointed Production Director.

With both companies being run by the same management team, turnover by 2009 is in excess of £34,000,000 and a production of approximately 85 million envelopes per week.

Today at any one time the Blackburn companies have in excess of 1,000 tonnes of various papers in stock. The production system is designed to ensure that the company can offer shorter lead-times than its competitors and still provide effectiveness and efficiency in the services it provides to all its customers.

Envelopes are clearly something we should never take for granted!

Top left: Inside the Heritage 100, 000 square foot purpose factory. Centre: Dedicated and professional staff ensure that the customers needs are always top priority. Below left, left to right: Martyn Salt, Logistics Director, Stuart Bromley, Finance Director and Ian Walmsley, Sales Director. Above right: Trevor Whittaker, Joint Managing Director. Below: Heritage Envelopes' Heritage House, Davyfield Road, premises.

WEC Group Ltd - Making Things Happen

Over the next eight years business grew from strength to strength. In 1987 the business became a limited company.

With employees and machinery now outgrowing Cranberry Lane, expansion was due and in 1992 the Company and its 100 employees moved to a 20,000 square feet site on Junction Street, Darwen. It was here that Ross decided to leave in order to concentrate on other interests, leaving Steve to run the Company. Over the next few years, another 35,000 square feet of premises was purchased to accommodate the growing business.

Today Darwen's WEC Group Ltd is one of the town's most prominent businesses. Its origins however were modest. The Welding Engineering Company was founded in 1979 by Steve Hartley and Ross Place, having both fallen victim to 'the three day week'. Following redundancy, Steve and Ross, both time-served tradesmen and in their early twenties, set out to provide a welding and fabrication service from a 1,000 square feet makeshift shed in Taylor Street, Darwen.

Business was steady, and by 1983 expansion was due. A fire at the plastics factory next door spurred the pair on to purchase a larger site on Cranberry Lane, Darwen. At a cost of £10,000, the business, now employing four people, moved to the 10,000 square feet, semi-derelict site, which required major work, but was just about affordable.

It was at Cranberry Lane that Steve and Ross' fortune changed. Approached by one of the first CCTV companies in the UK, they were asked to design and produce a camera tower. The pair accepted the project and set about designing the TW8 (the ST8 static 8m tower). The design was a success and from this small start the camera mounting side of the business was born.

Cranberry Lane was also the scene for the firm's second major contract, winning business to produce motorway poles for Philips (now TYCO). With this contract Steve and Ross were able to clear their debts and begin acquiring the additional necessary machinery and skills to increase productivity.

Technological advancements played a part in the next phase of the company's growth with the introduction of digital and laser technology. Steve took the plunge and bought the company's first laser cutting machine in 1998. Its capacity was soon reached however, and a second machine was purchased enabling the firm to provide a laser cutting service externally.

The growth of the company required a re-organisation of products and services into three divisions; Welding Engineering, Camera Mounting Solutions and Laser Engineering. The Company also changed from WEC Ltd to the WEC Group Ltd in 2003.

Still expanding rapidly, a new site was required to house stock, machinery and the 100 plus employees. In 2004 land was purchased on Spring Vale Road and a purpose-built facility was created for Welding Engineering covering 30,000 square feet. In 2006, an additional purpose-built office block and car park was added to the site.

In 2005, m-tec was set up to facilitate the demand for street architecture. Specialising in bespoke architectural metalwork and consultancy, m-tec works with architects, artists and councils on a number of urban regeneration projects and has been responsible for the Group's involvement in the design and manufacture of some of the most striking and unique pieces of street architecture in the UK.

At the end of 2005, Steve was approached by a local company, Precision Engineers, with an opportunity to purchase the machining company. As the Group was sub-contracting machining, it made sense to bring this in-house and, in December 2005, Precision Engineers was purchased along with another 15,000 square feet of space to house the division. Run as Precision Engineers for the next 18 months, the company re-branded the division as Hi-Spec CNC in 2007.

In 2006, the Group formed the WEC Welding & Engineering Academy, focusing on training apprentices in the skills of the trade. The apprentices are provided with the skills they require to compete effectively in the industry; the Academy is now going from strength to strength.

WEC Group Ltd now comprises six divisions; Welding Engineering, Camera Mounting Solutions, Laser Engineering, Hi-Spec CNC, m-tec and 5750 Components, acquired in October 2008. The Group is currently building

another 25,500 square feet purpose-built facility to increase much needed capacity.

Now with over 250 employees, the small welding and fabrication company set up in 1979 has become one of the largest suppliers in its field, a major employer in the local community and proud Darwen end stand sponsor of Blackburn Rovers Football Club for 2008 and 2009 season.

*Top left: WEC's Cranberry Lane site in the 1980s. **Bottom left:** Graduates at the Apprentice of the Year Awards 2008 with Andre Oojier, Dutch Defender for Blackburn Rovers and Instructor Kris Mercer. **Above:** Fabricated completely from stainless steel by m-tec, a division of WEC Group Ltd, this 75 tonne bridge was unveiled as the centrepiece of a £200 million regeneration scheme in Bristol. The unique £1.4 million, 200ft bridge links the city's Temple Quay harbour to the city centre. **Below:** An aerial view of WEC Group Ltd's Britannia House, Darwen, premises.*

Elco - On the Move

Based at the Oxford Works in Blackburn's Montague Street, Elco is a business which has over the course of more than half a century become internationally known and helped put Blackburn on the world map.

Founded in 1954, this long-established company specialises in the design and manufacture of purpose-built mechanical handling equipment – conveyor belts and similar machinery for moving goods and materials.

Primitive conveyor systems were used by the Romans. In 1901 a Swedish company invented and started the production of steel conveyor belts. In 1905 Richard Sutcliffe invented the first conveyor belts for use in coal mines, a development which revolutionised the mining industry. And in 1913, Henry Ford introduced a conveyor belt-based assembly-line in Ford Motor Company's Rouge factory, in Dearborne Michigan.

Today such equipment is to be found in almost every kind of industrial and commercial setting. For six decades Blackburn's Elco has been at the heart of that on-going evolution in industrial practice.

Elco, more formally known as the East Lancashire Conveyor Co Ltd (incorporated in 1956), would develop a broad customer base, servicing many clients in the chemical, steel, packaging, pulp and nuclear industries.

The firm was founded by Derek Taylor and Harold Jackson. Both were engineers who had previously worked on the design of conveyors; they had met in the late 1940s when Harold Jackson had joined the firm for which Derek was then working.

Both the engineers thought that there was a market for bespoke conveyors in industry and decided to try and meet that demand. Setting out to design bespoke mechanical handling equipment with innovative features for industry and heavy mineral supply companies began in a small way. Accommodation was rented in just a section of the Oxford Works. The pair could not imagine that they would eventually not only buy their premises but also extend into an adjacent section.

In the early days only Derek Taylor worked full-time, assisted by just one member of staff. Harold Jackson, with a young family to

offers a full in-house design, manufacture and test service, leading to on-site installation by its own skilled staff anywhere in the world. Clients can be found in Europe, Asia, Africa, America and Australia.

Facilities to manufacture and supply in conveyor component form, complete roller or full integrated roller systems have enabled the company to achieve a broad customer base, supplying clients in the packaging, food, paper and pulp, steel and other industries.

Elco realised the need for flexibility in the manufacture of gravity conveyors and their components due to the wide applications and industries where they are used. All types of conveyor rollers are manufactured including: Gravity rollers, Sprocketed rollers, Precision Idler rollers, Conveyor drums and Welded Conveyor rollers.

The firm's products are used in a vast variety of applications: car manufacturing, chemical processes, food production, paper products, electronic equipment, CDs, tyre manufacture, mortuary work and brewing.

Elco conveyors have been supplied to paper manufacturers in places as far apart as France and China. They are used by chocolate manufacturers in the USA, for plaster board production in Poland and Czechoslovakia, street lighting manufacture in Saudi Arabia and for heavy mineral extraction in Russia.

As for the future, Elco now aims to develop even more efficient and sophisticated mechanical handling systems to meet the 21st century needs of its customers around the world.

support, worked part-time in the evenings and at weekends whilst holding down another full-time job. Derek Taylor's father also worked as foreman in the 1950s and early 1960s.

A fabrication shop was built in Shaw Street in 1972, whilst in 1990 a further fabrication shop and office complex was added in Montague Street. Mr Peter S. Jackson, now the firm's Chairman, joined the business in 1973, followed in 1975 by Mr Peter Entwistle, the current Technical Director.

Derek Taylor retired in 1992. Harold Jackson had retired in 1983: sadly, he died in 2004 in the month following Elco's 50th anniversary.

Throughout more than half a century service and quality have been the touchstone for the company's products, and it is pleased to have been accredited with both a white and red area nuclear quality assured standard for manufacture.

Long experience has allowed the firm to bring together many different disciplines, as used in other industries, in the formulation of its designs for specific client's equipment. Elco

Top, facing page: A company outing to Blackpool in 1958.
Far left: The company's first conveyor belt at James Rothwell in Haslingden. Top left: Crate conveyors at Thwaites brewery in 1962. Above left: An Elco conveyor installed in a waste recycling plant in Wiltshire. Below: The company's Oxford Works premises in Montague Street.

BCP Fluted Packaging Ltd - Paper in the Blood

Today Blackburn's BCP Fluted Packaging Ltd is the epitome of a modern specialised packaging company, but the company's roots go back over a hundred years.

Isaac Crompton started his own business, The Waste Paper Company Limited, in Lord Street in 1903.

In 1909 Isaac moved from trading into manufacturing. He bought a second hand Bentley and Jackson paper machine and acquired a Smith and Law paper cutter along with other equipment which were installed in premises on Regent Street. At the same time Isaac changed the firm's name to The Richmond Hill Paper Company.

By the depression of the 1930s Isaac Crompton's son James was managing the Business. Given the tough economic climate he decided to 'vertically integrate' by investing in 'Corrugating' plant. As a result the Blackburn Corrugated Paper Co Ltd. was formed.

The new company started with one machine and a handful of staff in a former rifle range on Freme Street. The premises had been built in 1909 by the Hornby family, whose coat of arms can still be seen on the façade. James Crompton's young nephew, Edward Crompton Jones, was now drafted in to help.

Throughout the Second World War both Companies had continued to trade, though production was limited to work supporting the war effort. In 1942 James Crompton's son Roland started at the Paper Mill, then, following his father's untimely death at fifty three in 1944, his Uncle Gwynne Jones, a retired teacher from Bolton School, joined the Board. Gwynne's second son, Harry Jones joined in 1946.

Top left: *A young Edward Jones pictured outside Blackburn Corrugated (circa 1933) with a horse-drawn cart in the background making local deliveries of corrugated rolls.* **Left:** *Chief Constable G. Looms empties sets of finger prints in Richmond Hill's pulp, watched to his left by Roland Crompton, grandson of the founder Isaac Crompton.* **Above:** *The aftermath of the fire in 1958.*

One of the most unusual events in the Company's history came in 1948. The murder of four-year-old June Anne Devaney had appalled Blackburn. The entire town's male adult population, 46,000, were finger printed on the proviso that all sets taken would later be destroyed. Blackburn Corrugated Paper subsequently converted them into corrugated paper.

Ten years later, in 1958, a fire at the Paper Mill ripped through the four storey building. Amazingly the paper machine on the ground floor survived, despite it taking twelve hours for the fire brigade to extinguish the flames. Richmond Hill Paper's main purpose from then on was to provide fluting paper for the corrugating Business.

Blackburn Corrugated diversified into the niche markets of corrugating and embossing specialised papers used for confectionery and bakery.

By the time the Company was celebrating its 50th anniversary in 1980 it had 150 staff with fourteen small corrugating and embossing machines and an annual turnover of £5 million.

Edward Jones' son David was now running the corrugating Business, with his cousin Michael, Harry's eldest son, as Sales Director. Families also ran through the works, with many old staff members' sons, daughters and even grand children in the business.

The recession of the late 1980s proved tough and Richmond Hill Paper Mill finally ceased production in March 1989. The old mill's foundations are now below the Barbara Castle Way inner ring road. Happily 'Blackburn Corrugated' proved more resilient, developing additional niche products, including fine fragrance packaging supplied to major brands like Estée Lauder, Elizabeth Arden and Avon Cosmetics.

However, as the 20th century drew to a close competition was beginning to have a serious impact on profitability.

In 1999, with the future of the Business in doubt, Harry Jones's youngest son Brian, who had not previously been involved with the company, acquired a controlling interest. Assisted by his brother Michael and his half cousin Lee, who represents the fifth generation, Brian, set about changing the direction and fortunes of the Business.

Today the firm's long history is reflected in the name given to a new 8,000 square metre factory, 'Crompton House', built off Nuttalls Way on Shadsworth Business Park in 2006.

Only two machines survive from the ones Brian Jones acquired seven years earlier. The plant is dominated by a new corrugating machine with modern converting machines to process a range of specialised fluted products. Gone are the traditional brown packaging products, replaced by sophisticated food packaging and fragrance liners. To reflect the changes the name of the business also changed: BCP Fluted Packaging Ltd is now recognised as a leading innovator in 'Corrugated' throughout Europe. Turnover is approaching £10 million.

Brian Jones and his team are proud of the Company's traditions and have laid firm foundations for its future.

Above: A view inside the new Crompton House factory, 2008.
Below: Lee, Michael and Brian Jones outside the Company's premises which was named in recognition of the original founder Isaac Crompton.

Presspart Manufacturing - It's in the Can

It's an amazing fact, but the aerosol canisters used in half the world's asthma inhalers are made in Blackburn. Each year hundreds of millions of cans are produced by Presspart Manufacturing Ltd based on the Whitebirk Industrial Estate.

In the early 1990s the company employed some 240 staff in Blackburn; today, following massive increases in efficiency, there are around 140 employees.

Presspart began life in 1970. Its founders were Tony Hutchinson, Bob Watts and Tony Cann. Tony Hutchinson hoped to start his own business and was looking for an investor. Tony Cann was an established businessman in the Blackburn area, who met Tony Hutchinson in a pub in the village of Grindleton where they both lived. Tony Cann expressed an interest in supporting Tony Hutchinson, provided that he had a partner to help with sales. This was how Bob Watts, previously a colleague of Tony Hutchinson's at Neotechnic Engineering in Clitheroe, came into the picture.

Another key figure, and one of the longest serving individuals in the company's history, would be Tom Pattinson who joined the company in 1971 as a toolmaker; he retired in 2007 having held the positions of Production Manager, Works Manager, Manufacturing Director and Engineering Director.

Presspart began business manufacturing 'deep-drawn' metal components for a variety of industries.

The company commenced operations at 'Hilltop Works', the first factory unit erected on the Whitebirk Industrial Estate in 1970. Today the factory buildings have expanded to occupy some 9,250 square metres.

Tony Hutchinson was Technical Director and Bob Watts the Commercial Director. Tony Cann, as the principal shareholder, was Chairman.

The company started with two small 'Platarg' multi-stage deep-draw presses, bought second-hand. At the peak of battery can and writing instrument component manufacturing there were some 80 Platarg presses in use. Today 40 modern presses produce components at 3-4 times the rate of the first machines.

Presspart would excel at producing complicated shaped components from a

Above: Founders, Bob Watts (left) and Tony Hutchinson.
Bottom: The company's first Hilltop premises in 1971.
Right: Presspart hit the headlines in 1988 when Works Director Alex Anderson collected the prestigious 1987 North West Business and Industry Award on behalf of Presspart.

range of metals. One sales engineer, when asked by a customer if a part could be made from a particular metal, used to joke that it could be made out of alligator skin if that could be purchased in coils!

Presspart expanded in 1975 when a sister company, Decorpart Ltd, was established in Nelson to produce anodised aluminium pressings for the pharmaceutical and cosmetics industry. Presspart was awarded the Queen's Award for Export in 1983, and would become the first company in its field to achieve the BS 5750 quality management system certification.

John Czarnecki, originally a design engineer and credited with the design of the Eubank carpet sweeper, became Works Manager and later Works Director, before leaving to become Managing Director of Decorpart in 1984, a position he held until his retirement in 1990.

Alex Anderson, also a former tool design engineer, became Works Director in 1984, Managing Director in 1991 and in 1993 became the Vice President and General Manager of Presspart Inc. before retiring in 1995.

Presspart was sold to the Rockware Group plc in 1988, following which Tony Cann took a seat on the Rockware board and Tony Hutchinson became Chief Executive of the Rockware Group Metals Division (Rockware was principally a manufacturer of glass bottles and jars for food and beverages). Presspart Inc. in North Carolina in the USA was founded in 1988 as a sales and distribution business. In 1993,

however, a purpose built factory was established to produce metered-dose inhaler (MDI) cans for the American market.

The Rockware Group was subsequently broken up, and Presspart and Decorpart were acquired by a management buy-out team in 1994.

Two years earlier Bob Watts died, along with three other local businessmen, whilst flying to Scotland. Tony Cann and Tony Hutchinson ended their association with the company after the break-up of the Rockware Group.

Presspart was acquired by the Heitkamp and Thumann Group in 2002. The company's plant in the USA was closed in 2006 and production transferred back to Blackburn.

Today Presspart's main customers are the world's leading pharmaceutical companies which it supplies with canisters for metered-dose inhalers for the treatment of asthma and chronic obstructive pulmonary disease.

The company now produces some 300 million cans each year (around 50% of the world's demand), with a further 150-200 million cans being produced at the Presspart plant in Germany. Presspart also has a plant in Tarragona, Spain, producing plastic actuator/mouthpieces for metered dose inhalers.

Top left: A view of the factory in 1990 clearly shows how the company had constantly expanded since the early years.
Centre: Examples of products manufactured by Presspart.
Below: Presspart's premises in 2009.

Parkinson Signs - Signs of the Times

Perhaps the biggest difference between the 19th and the 20th century was the arrival of electric lighting. One of Blackburn's longest established family-owned businesses is Parkinson Signs Ltd based at the Chapel Street works. And it's a company which has done more than most to brighten Blackburn.

The firm was founded by Arnold Parkinson in 1946.

Having formerly trained as an electrician, Arnold had earlier worked at the Star Paper Mill, and then, during the war, at Mullard's.

Joined by an ex-Mullard's work colleague and friend, John Worden, the business which would become Parkinson & Worden Ltd first operated from the front room of No. 29 Brothers Street. In 1948 they moved to 49 King Street, next to the old Court House, where their workshop expanded and the business grew to employ eight people, including Alan Walmsley and William Lightbown. These two employees remained in Parkinson & Worden service through to their retirements in 1998 and 1997 respectively.

In the early days the majority of business was making neon and cold cathode tube signs, this later expanded to cover a wider aspect of signage.

Some of the large names such as Spiller Flour Mills and Walker's Steel were illuminated by Parkinson's lighting. Arnold Parkinson liked to reminisce how the famous local businessman Jack Walker of Walker's Steel (later to become one of Britain's richest

men and benefactor of Blackburn Rovers), delivered steel to Parkinson & Worden by horse and hand cart in his early days.

In 1960 the business moved to 12/14 Chapel Street, a former Hindle Saw Mill, which is still the Company base today. Expansion over a period of time included the purchase of cottages on Freckleton Street and Chapel Street to further increase the size of the business premises.

In the early 1960s one of Blackburn's most notable landmarks was created by Parkinson & Worden – the illuminated Thwaites

tower's ten-foot-high letters. This was a very prestigious contract which the Company is still proud of, and the large letters are still maintained by Parkinson's today.

In 1969 John Worden left the business and Arnold's son, Gordon Parkinson, joined the family firm from a previous background in electrical engineering. The business continued to expand

Above: Founder, Arnold Parkinson. Below: Walkers & Sons signage by Parkinsons in the 1970s. Above right: Gordon Parkinson. Right: Thwaites tower's ten foot high lettering created by Parkinsons.

In the following years the firm continued to forge an enviable reputation in Blackburn.

Down the decades the firm has consistently embraced the most modern technology, but whilst updating machinery and processes it has done so without sacrificing old fashioned quality and a close attention to customer service.

In 2005, as part of a modernisation of the Company image, the name of Parkinson & Worden Ltd was changed to the simpler, more direct Parkinson Signs Ltd.

Gordon Parkinson retired in 2007 leaving the firm in the hands of Ian Parkinson.

Many of the firm's clientele are still in the same or related businesses as they were 40 years ago or more. In 2009, Parkinsons provided a new image for Edmondson's Furniture on Darwen Street, another long standing local family firm.

Today, Parkinson Signs is a company proud of its heritage; it looks forward to not only sustaining, but enhancing, the reputation for excellence handed down from its founders to the present generation.

Top left and above left: Signs created by Parkinsons for Dutton's and the Saxon Inn. Left: Ian Parkinson, Managing Director, 2009. Below: Parkinson Signs Chapel Street Works premises.

and found a wide market in the brewing industry sector, specialising in signage on public houses for local brewers such as Whitbreads (formerly Thomas Duttons), Matthew Brown (formerly Nuttalls) and Thwaites – of which, sadly, only Thwaites' brewery still remains in the town.

The firm now started to specialise in other areas of signage, not least for the banking sector, obtaining national contracts with both Natwest and TSB banks.

Parkinson & Worden went from strength to strength, eventually employing up to 35 people but still keeping its loyalty to staff of many years service, such as Brian Fray and Albert Taylor, who eventually retired with a combined total of 54 years' service.

Company founder, Arnold Parkinson, died in 1986. This left the firm solely in the hands of his son Gordon. Arnold's grandson Ian Parkinson subsequently joined the company straight from school at the age of 18 and proceeded to learn the business from the ground up – starting as a delivery driver – and eventually working his way up to the post of Managing Director.

Acknowledgments

The publishers would like to pay special and sincere thanks to the following individuals and organisations for their help and contribution to make this publication possible

Diana Rushton, Community History Manager
for Blackburn with Darwen Library

Lancashire Telegraph
with particular thanks to Neil Johnson, Picture Editor

National Monuments Record (NMR), the public archive
of English Heritage. For further information about these
aerial images please telephone: 01793 414600 or email:
nmrinfo@english-heritage.org.uk

Jim Halsall Collection